CW00572604

Stress Management & Burnout

The Ultimate Guide to Manage Stress and Avoid Burnout in Your Life

Declan Evans

Table of Contents

Stress Management 9
Introduction 10
Chapter 1: What is Stress? 12
Types of Stress 16
Chapter 2: Stress or Anxiety? 21
Health Problems 25
Psychological Effects 27
Behavioral Effects 27
Cognitive Effects 28
Positive Effects of Stress 29
How to Block The Behaviors Keeping Your Stress Alive 29
Chapter 3: Stress and Your Self-Esteem 32
The Stress/Self-Esteem Cycle 32
Build Self-Esteem by Demolishing Excess Stress 33
Seeing Green 37
Do One Thing All the Way 38
Commit to Yourself 41
Chapter 4: Motivate Your Groundbreaking Resolve to Dig Down to the Roots of Your Stressed Energy 43
Layout a success foundation – in your mind! 43
Work on your willpower 44
Your willpower: the power of an indomitable persistence 45
So, what is willpower? 45
Why do you need willpower? 46
What breeds willpower? 47
How do you boost your willpower? 48
How to use life quotes to fire up the motivation you need to radically change your life? 50

Chapter 5: Approaching the Exercises 54
Major Life Change Checklist 54
Set the Stage 56
State Your Goals 57
Choose Your Exercises 59
Your Physical Needs 59
Your Physical Self-Care Values 62
Physical Self-Care Activities 63
Time to Engage 65
Create a Physical Self-Care Schedule 65
Chapter 6: Mindfulness 67
Meditation: The Foundation of Mindfulness 67
Mindful Morning Meditation 69
Meditation for a Stressful Day 70
Learning the Role of Impartial Observer 70
The Key To Well-Being 73
Creating A Relationship With Yourself 75
Building Your Mindfulness Muscle 77
Chapter 7: Overcoming Stress 78
Chapter 8: Change Your Stress Environment 84
Soul Healing Meditations 84
Be Happy and Joyful 86
How to Develop a Merry Heart Laughter 87
Practice Forgiveness 88
Take control of your tongue 88
Surround yourself with positive friends 88
Spend time with loved ones 89
Connect with Nature 89
Take Time to be Grateful 89

Feed Your Mind with Positive Thoughts 90
Belly Breathing 90
Exhale through your mouth. As you exhale, you should feel your abdomen begin to fall. 91
Maintain a regular breathing schedule 92
Chapter 9: Inner Happiness 93
Chapter 10: Tips for Building Self-Social Confidence 101
Strategies For Improving Your Social Confidence 106
Conclusion 111
Burnout 117
Introduction 118
Types of Burnout 119
Burnout sign and symptoms 120
Method 1: *Talk to your Family Doctor* 122
He/she runs things like a tight ship 122
Family Physician 123
What family doctor can do about burnout? 125
Method 2: *See a Psychologist* 127
Reasons to see a psychologist cure burnout 127
Counseling session for burnout 128
Method 3: *Do Yoga* 130
Yoga 130
Different Types of Yoga 131
Yoga at home 133
Yoga as part of a workout routine 134
Benefits of Yoga for burnout 134
Is Yoga for Burnout right for you? 135
Method 4: *Praise Mindfulness Meditation* 136
Why Meditate? 136
Mindfulness Meditation for Burnout 136

Mindfulness Therapy for Burnout 137
Mindfulness and Burnout 138
But how do I get started? 140
Method 5: *Get a Massage* 142
Why do you need a massage? 142
Benefits of massage for burnout 143
Method 6: Practice Art Therapy 147
Art Therapy 147
Creative Ways to Deal with Burnout 147
Art Therapy and Burnout 151
Method 7: *Try acupuncture* 153
Does Acupuncture Work for Stress and Burnout? 153
Acupuncture and Burnout 153
Asking for Acupuncture 154
Method 8: *Exercise* 158
Why Exercise? 159
Aerobic Exercise (Level 1/Low Intensity) 160
Active recovery (Level 2/Moderate Intensity) 160
Physical activity breaks (Level 3/High Intensity) 160
Before you exercise... 160
Body awareness and relaxation 161
Method 9: *Cut Down on Caffeine Consumption* 163
What is Caffeine? 163
Health Concerns 164
Caffeine and Burnout 165
The Effects of Caffeine on the Brain 167
Bad Effects of Too Much Caffeine 168
Bad Habits of Taking Caffeine 168
Caffeine Alternatives 168

Method 10: *Rest when on Leave* 170
Rest to Prevent Burnout 170
How to get a good night's rest 171
Strategies to Help You Rest from Burnout 172
Benefits of resting 172
Method 11: *Set Boundaries* 174
Boundaries and Burnout 176
How to draw boundaries 177
Once you set a boundary, hold firm 178
Method 12: *Practice Self-compassion* 181
Benefits 181
How to Practice Self-Compassion 182
Why We Need to Practice Self-Compassion 183
Method 13: *Remember What Makes You Happy* 185
Method 14: *Learn to Say "no"* 189
Why it's So Difficult to Say no? 189
Avoid Burnout and Start Saying No. Here's How. 190
Saying No Guilt-free 193
Method 15: *Learn to Delegate* 196
What is Delegation? 196
Delegation in the Workplace 196
Delegation Tips 197
Delegating Effectively 197
Doing and Delegating 199
How to Delegate Effectively 200
Getting in the Right Mindset 201
Importance of being a delegate 201
Why Delegate? 202
Method 16: *Get Enough Sleep* 204

How Sleep Helps Burnout? 204
Having Trouble Sleeping? 206
How to Improve Sleep Hygiene 209
Method 17: *Eat Well* 211
Essential to Eat Well 211
How much should you eat? 211
Is There a Stress Management Diet? 212
Foods for Stress Relief 213
Method 18: *Take Time for Yourself - Guilt-free* 216
Guilt-Free Ways to Make Time for Yourself 216
Method 19: *Get Support from Loved Ones* 222
Seek family advice 222
Ask Friends for Help 223
Meditation 223
Professional help 223
Method 20: *Work Part-time* 225
Working Part-time 225
Be Productive 229
Stay Creative 229
Method 21: *Change jobs* 231
Job Burnout 231
Possible causes of job burnout 232
Getting Past Burnout at Work 234
Take a break 236
Change your job to escape burnout 236
Method 22: *Get to the Root of the Problem* 238
Identifying the root cause of the problem 238
Eliminating the root cause 241
Conclusion 243

Stress Management

Beating Stress is Easier Than You Think

Declan Evans

Introduction

Life is full of difficulties, and people need to share in these moments. Imagine being alone and not having someone else to vent to or celebrate with. This alone can be stressful without adding the real cause of the stress. Experts say that sharing problems with other people provides resilience to overcome those problems. However, when people encounter stress daily, the body responds to the stress the same way it would respond to any other harmful stimuli in its environment.

When the body comes in contact with stress regularly, it stores the stress hormones instead of the normal response of releasing them throughout the body. These hormones become a problem when stored, and the body decides to get rid of them the production of stomach ulcers, anxiety, and insomnia.

Developing effective stress management skills can help a person better handle tough situations and make them more manageable. It can also make a person more aware of what stressors face them to help the person avoid them. The key is to know what types of stress are out there and how to deal with them.

"Stress is the state of being put to strain." In American society, anxiety is a common problem that has serious health, social, and emotional effects on people of all ages and backgrounds. Various factors can cause stress; some include risks, demands, and concerns.

The body, for example, gets inflammations ready in case of injury and infection. It signals the body to have a “fight or flight” reaction.

Frequent reactions like this can lead to serious illnesses like cancer. Stress also weakens the immune system and makes it hard for the body to fight disease and illness.

Chapter 1:
What is Stress?

Stress is the natural reaction of your body and mind to dangerous, anxiety-inducing situations. When you feel threatened or stressed, your body will release hormones that in turn will make you alert and prepared to react to any emergency you may encounter. In psychology, this is the "fight or flight" response that occurs in both humans and animals. The problem is that our bodies do not distinguish if the stressor is a crazed wild bear, a deadline at work, a car accident, or a calculus test. It reacts to all of the above, and even little things, like a hangnail or a glass of spilled milk, in the exact same way.

So how exactly does your body react to stress? Chances are, you have felt it all before though you might have called it something like a panic or an anxiety attack: your muscles tighten, your heart beats faster, you might get a little sweaty, and your senses, particularly your hearing and sense of smell, get sharper. You are ready for action, and usually that action is to run. These reactions make it easier to fight or flee, but adults can't always fight or flee their stressors as they are necessary to keep your life on track. Skipping out on your stressors for even a day can add to much more stress. Instead, you are stuck feeling tense and overwhelmed while creating even more stressors in your life. However, not all stress is actually bad stress.

The Science Behind Stress

The stress response starts within the brain. A stress signal is sent to the hypothalamus, which then messages the nervous system to protect you from the threat. This then influences the nervous system to begin increasing your heart rate to get you ready for fight or flight mode. Due to this, all your blood rushes to your muscles to get you ready to defend yourself, which then slows down the other functions of the body. This includes your digestive secretions, intestines, and your body begins to flood with cortisol. When your body reacts this way too often, it begins to cause significant physical damage. Whenever there is too much cortisol running through your brain for extended amounts of time, hippocampal brain damage begins to occur. This causes people to have a disturbed sleep cycle, memory loss, mood swings, and they always feel not "all there" due to the brain fog.

The pituitary gland also becomes affected during stress responses. Its responsibility is to regulate bodily functions such as thyroid activity, urine production, and body temperature. When people are nervous or anxious, they feel like they have to use the bathroom frequently. During times of high stress, cortisol is produced from these glands and pulls fat and glucose from the body into the bloodstream for energy. This is why during acute stress a lot of people feel like they don't have an appetite.

The heart is another organ that is heavily affected during high-stress times. Blood vessels become constricted, which makes it difficult for the heart to pump blood properly. People begin to have high blood pressure due to the smaller blood vessels. In addition, your adrenal glands are heavily affected when your body detects stress. It signals your adrenal glands to release adrenaline and noradrenaline into your body. These hormones are responsible for increasing both blood pressure and heart rate. Due to your blood being pumped into your extremities, it produces a feeling of butterflies in your stomach. When this process happens frequently and does not leave you time to recuperate, you begin to feel wound up and tired at the same time, almost like the feeling of drinking coffee but still feeling tired along with a racing heart. When people go through stress too often, the stress wears out the adrenal glands, which can lead to exhaustion, depression, physical weakness, immune suppression, skin problems, and hormone imbalances long term.

A person's stomach and digestive system are heavily affected when under stress as the blood is being pulled to other parts of your body. When your digestive system is slowed down due to this process, your digestive acids can either be overproduced, which will lead to acid reflux, or under-produced, which means your stomach has lower digestive power. When a person has too little stomach acid, the food in their belly actually ferments rather than digests, which creates bloating.

Although people report stress that helped them lose weight and even helped some gain weight, research has found high levels of cortisol encourages weight gain. Cortisol increases a person's appetite for fast energy, creating cravings for sugar and carbohydrates. It also creates extra glucose in a person's body, and when it's not burned off through exercise, this extra glucose gets stored as fat. Being under chronic stress is the true enemy of overall fitness. People tend to gain weight because their cravings are stronger, making it more likely that you hold onto food as fat, especially in the abdominal area.

The reproductive system is also affected when under stress as the increased production of cortisol causes a lower production of progesterone, a fertility hormone in women. When the amount is lowered, it leads to possible infertility and a low libido. When people are under a lot of stress, they don't want to engage in sexual activity.

Stress Checklist

Are you always hiding what you truly think or feel because you do not want other to hear people's opinions, or you might be afraid of their reactions? You have got to speak your truth and stop worrying about what the outcome. That causes tremendous stress, anxiety as well as depression, and it messes with your self-esteem. The following is a checklist for you to see where some of your stress is coming from.

Do you fear that letting people in and letting them know what you are doing will make them criticize you or use it against you later?

Do you only focus on negative things, violent movies, violent videos, instead of normal and loving things?

Are you afraid to ask for things in your relationship because you are constantly being told you are too demanding, or you think they will ask what is wrong with you?

Do you feel comfortable actually addressing your partner with your needs and wants?

Do you have friends, family, or a partner that is always denying you, degrading you, or putting you down?

Does your point of view matter to the people around you?

Are you constantly made to feel like you can never do anything right?

You cannot possibly feel good or fulfilled by holding back because if you were self-confident, you would not have a problem asking for what you want. This is something to work on immediately.

These are all things that cause heavy amounts of stress because anytime you are walking around carrying fear and pressure about something, it is going to cause you to be stressed!

Types of Stress

As you may already know, there are different types or levels of stress. The stress you feel before writing an exam compared to the stress that you feel when you are going through a traumatic experience is very different. The frequency of the stress you feel also plays a huge factor in the type of stress you have. There are three types, according to the APA (American Psychological Association). These are acute stress, episodic acute stress, and chronic stress.

Each of these stress types has its own duration, symptoms, characteristics, and treatments. This is why stress management is very complicated. The three stress types can also be in the form of complicated, repeated, single, or chronic. It comes down to the individual's lifestyle, environment, coping resources, personality, and developmental history.

Let's take a look into the three different types:

1. Acute Stress

This type of stress is typically very brief and is the most common stress type. It tends to happen frequently, and reactive thinking is the cause.

A person can have negative thoughts dominating their mind in situations that occurred recently that affect future situations (for instance, if a person has recently been in a quarrel, they may begin to have stress that related to the negative thoughts going on in their mind). They may be having acute stress regarding an upcoming deadline, which is also induced through thoughts. However, when a person changes those negative thoughts into something more positive or if they reduce the frequency of those negative thoughts, their stress will begin to subside as well.

Here are some of the common signs of acute stress:

Transient stomach problems; heartburn, constipation, diarrhea, flatulence, acid stomach, and any gut and bowel problems.

Transient muscular distress; headache, tension, back pain, jaw pain, neck pain, and any muscular tension.

Transient emotional distress; a combination of irritability or anger, and anxiety, and depression.

Transient hyperarousal, rapid pulse, shortness of breath, increased heartbeat, increased blood pressure, dizziness, migraines, sleep problems, chest pain, heart palpitations, and cold hands/feet.

Episodic Acute Stress

Persons experiencing acute stress frequently, or living a life full of stressors, are more likely to have episodic acute stress. These people tend to live in a life of crisis and chaos. They feel pressured all the time and are always in a rush. They may take on too many responsibilities but struggle with staying organized when there are too many deadlines. There are two main types of personalities more likely to have this type of stress. The first type is anyone with an "A" type personality, and the second type is the 'worrier.'

People who have Type A personalities tend to be very competitive, abrupt, aggressive, impatient, and have a strong sense of urgency. They also tend to be insecure about their performance and feel the need to be perfect every time. People with such traits often create episodes of stress for themselves frequently. Due to this, scientists have found that people with a Type A' personality have a higher likelihood of developing heart disease later on in life.

The worrier type constantly has negative thoughts that cause stress on their mental and physical health. These types are always projecting disasters or negatively assuming a catastrophe throughout their lives. They tend to believe that the world is a very dangerous place where a bad things will always happen to them. These people have a lot of negative thoughts that make them depressed and anxious. They are more likely to be diagnosed with GAD (generalized anxiety disorder).

Here are some of the symptoms of the episodic effects of acute stress:

Immune system compromise (ISC), constantly getting allergies, flu, colds, and other types of illnesses related to ISC.

Stomach issues, irritable bowel syndrome (IBS), constipation, diarrhea, flatulence, acid stomach, heartburn, bowel problems, and gut problems.

High blood pressure, migraines, rapid heartbeat, dizziness, insomnia, heart disease, heart palpitations, and cold hands/feet

Muscular distress, ligament problems, tendons, pulled muscles, jaw pain, back pain, headaches, and body tension

Deterioration of interpersonal relationships, the workplace becomes too stressful.

Cognitive distress, mental fatigue, compromised new learning abilities, compromised processing speed, compromised attention, and concentration.

Emotional distress in the form of tenseness, impatience, short-tempered, depression, anxiety, irritability, and anger issues.

Chronic Stress

This type of stress is the most harmful of the three. When it is not treated for an extended amount of time, chronic stress can cause damage to your mental and physical health irreversibly. For instance, unhappy marriage, repeated abuse in any form, poor work environments, long-term poverty, unemployment, or dysfunctional family can cause this type of stress.

When a person feels hopeless and sees no way out, and they give up entirely on finding solutions. Stress can set in and begin affecting their physical and mental health. When a person continuously lives with this type of stress, their emotional and behavioral actions can become ingrained. The wiring of their body and brain begins to change, making them more prone to negative effects that put stress on the body regardless of what's actually happening at the moment.

Chronic stress is a grinding type of stress because it wears people down day after day. It negatively impacts the body and mind in a significant way and has the power to change a person forever. Chronic stress can be so dangerous that it can kill people due to suicide, heart attacks, strokes, and even cancer. treatment practices can help manage chronic stress, but it requires them to be actively practicing certain techniques throughout their lives.

If you think you are someone who is suffering from chronic stress, get help right away. Seek professional opinion and get diagnosed. It will be the first step in discovering what methods are most suitable for your type of stress. In some cases, you may not even have chronic stress and just another type. In that case, different methods and techniques will be pursued to manage it properly.

Chapter 2:
Stress or Anxiety?

In contrary to popular belief, there is a contrast between stress and anxiety. Stress originates from the pressures we feel in life, as we are pushed by work or whatever reasons, and some are clearly unjustifiable. This releases adrenaline and the lengthy visit of this hormone cause depression, a rise in blood pressures and other negatives changes and effects.

One of the negative effects is anxiety. With anxiety, fear overcomes all emotions joined by worry and apprehension, making an individual a recluse and bagful of jitters. Other indications are chest pain, dizziness, and shortness of breath, and panic attacks.

Stress is brought about by existing stress-causing factors or stressors. While anxiety is the stress that proceeds after that stressor is no more, stress can emerge from any circumstances or thoughts that makes you feel frustrated, angry, and nervous, even anxious. What is stressful to one individual may not be really stressful to another.

Anxiety is a feeling of dread or apprehension and is quite often joined by feelings of impending doom. The source of this uneasiness isn't constantly known or perceived, which can add to the distress you feel. Stress is the manner in which our bodies and minds respond to the things which upset our ordinary, normal, balanced life; an example is when we are feeling threatened or frightened.

During stressful occasions, our adrenal organs discharge adrenaline; this hormone activates the body's protection system, which makes our heart pound faster, causes a rise in blood pressure, tense muscles, and the dilation of pupils. A key sign of increment stress is the acceleration in pulse rate; however, having a normal pulse rate doesn't really imply you aren't stressed.

Steady chronic pains and aches, chronic fatigue, anxiety, crying, over or under eating, frequent infections, and a decrease in sexual drive are signs you might be under stress. Obviously, every time we are under stress, we don't need to respond as if it is an extraordinary state, and we may not always be under great duress or fear every time we are faced with a stressful circumstance.

A few people are more vulnerable than others to stress. For some individuals, even ordinary daily decisions seem to be difficult. Choosing what to have for supper or what to purchase at the store is a seemingly monumental dilemma for them. Then again, there are those who appear to flourish under stress by turning out to be exceptionally productive.

Studies shows that women with children have a more significant level of stress-related hormones in their blood than women without kids. Does this mean women without children don't encounter stress? Absolutely not! it implies that women without children may not encounter stress as regularly or in a similar way than women with children. For women with children, it's particularly important to schedule time for yourself so you can be in a better frame of mind to meet the daily challenge of being a parent while anxiety, on the other hand, is a feeling of unease everybody experience when faced with a stressful circumstance.

For instance, before a test or interview or during a worrying time such as sickness. It's entirely normal to feel anxious when confronting something risky or difficult, and mild anxiety can be a good and helpful experience. Notwithstanding, for some individuals anxiety meddles with their ordinary life. Getting anxious excessively is frequently connected with other mental conditions, such as depression.

Anxiety is considered abnormal when it's very prolonged or extreme, it occurs without a stressful occasion, or it's interfering with everyday activities such as going to work. The physical symptoms of anxiety are caused by the brain sending messages to the parts of the body to prepare for a "fight or flight" reaction. The hearts, lungs, and other parts of the body then start to work quicker. The brain also releases stress hormones, including adrenaline.

Common indicators of excessive anxiety are:

Diarrhea

Dry mouth

Insomnia

Anger

Fear of being crazy

Feeling unreal and not in control of one action called "depersonalizations."

Rapid heartbeat

Anxiety can be brought on in various ways. Obviously, the presence of stress in your life can cause you to have anxious thoughts. Many individuals who experience the ill effects of anxiety issues occupy their minds with excessive worry. This can be worrying over anything from health matters to job and world issues. Certain drugs, both recreational and therapeutic, can also cause symptoms of anxiety due to either side effects or withdrawal from the medications. Such drugs include caffeine, alcohol, nicotine, cold remedies, and decongestants, tricyclic, bronchodilators for asthma, cocaine, diet pills, ADHD medications, and thyroid drugs.

A poor diet can likewise add to anxiety or stress, for instance, low degrees of vitamin B12.

Performance anxiety is related to specific circumstances, like taking a test or making an open introduction. Post-traumatic stress disorder (PTSD) is a stress disorder that develops after a traumatic like war, physical assault, or a natural disaster.

In very uncommon cases, a tumor of the adrenal organ (pheochromocytoma) might be the reason for anxiety. This happens because of an overproduction of hormones responsible for the feelings and symptoms of anxiety.

While anxiety may appear to be somewhat frightening, what's significantly more terrifying is that excessive anxiety and stress can lead to depression can be a long-lasting fight, but fortunately, all this is manageable.

Effects of Stress

Stress has various impacts on an individual body. These impacts might be physical, emotional, behavioral, and even mental. Stress has both positive and negative impacts; positive impacts are acceptable; however, you need to keep an eye out for the negative impacts since they can be hazardous to the point of being threatening.

Health Problems

Stress can enormously influence your wellbeing. This ordinarily happens when the stress level turns crazy. There are various medical issues that are straightforwardly connected to stress.

Acute or chronic pains can be brought upon by stress; one of the most widely recognized pain is migraine. An individual is possibly having a serious headache that the cause is indefinable; this headache might be chronic or acute.

Another common pain is chest pain; somebody may encounter a pain in the chest that can be painful. There additionally individuals who experience sharp agony in the stomach. All this pain can't be treated by medicine.

Medication may just offer transitory relief; to eliminate the pain, it is essential to move away from the stressor. Stress may likewise cause pain from different sicknesses to feel much worse. For instance, a stress cancer patient may easily experience very severe pains.

Stress may likewise cause serious health problems such as heart diseases; it also influence how the heart works; a stressed individual can develop a heart attack when they heard the sudden bad news. This shows that the individual has been exposed to a high stress level that their bodies can’t deal with it. Living with steady stress may cause heart issues.

Stress can also cause obesity. Many people who like to eat a lot when they are stressed, while there are others turn to their "comfort nourishments," which most of the time is junk food. This may make a stressed individual achieve quick weight gain, and again there are people who begin to experience a lack of appetite. They start skipping meals or eating less, which will deprive the body of essential nutrients and may bring about diet deficiency sickness. It also weakens the body's immune systems making one very susceptible to become sick.

Stomach-related issues may likewise be handily experienced. A stressed individual may begin feeling constipated, while others may start having diarrhea. It likewise causes a sleeping disorder; each individual needs to get sufficient rest in order to keep their bodies solid and functioning well. Insomnia can cause more health problems.

In addition, it will repress an individual's capacities to proceed with their day-by-day schedules. While some start sleeping a lot when they are stressed, some even have trouble keeping their eyes open at work or school. Individual may feel fatigued and sleepy at all times.

One of the most genuine impacts of stress is depression, which can greatly affect the quality of individual life; the afflicted will feel distanced from others and may even beginning separating themselves. This will definitely have a very negative impact on their relationships. A stressed individual may also start encountering the feeling of hopelessness. They may give up on life, and this is very risky.

Study shows that the significant reason for suicide is depression, while stress also causes blood pressure related issues. It can make blood pressure go really high or low; in addition, people who have had previous problems with blood pressure can get serious complications due to stress. Any stressful occurrence will make their circulatory strain go up to the levels that can be dangerous.

Stress also causes skin problems, such as acne. Stressed individual skin will also start looking unhealthy and lose its natural glow. Individuals who are stressed tend to look almost ten years older than they actually are. Their skin normally loses that young fresh look.

Psychological Effects

Stress will make an individual lose their self-esteem; they begin to feel they are not equivalent to other people. They may even feel like life has been remorseless to them and that they deserve more. An individual who has an issue in getting a job may easily stress. This can happen especially if they see that everybody around them is prevailing in their own careers.

They may begin to believe that they do lack what others have; they may also start feeling like they will never be able to accomplish their objectives. A stressed individual will consistently feel exceptionally pessimistic about existence; this individual will not be able to think positively.

They may lose enthusiasm for the quest for their fantasies; such individuals may start withdrawing from others. They may start abandoning things that they enjoy doing before, e.g., a stressed artist may abruptly lose interest in art and adopt the "what's the point" attitude. Which means everything seems to have lost its value in their eyes.

Behavioral Effects

Most people turn to alcohol consumption excessively, use of hard drugs, etc. they only use this as an escapism strategy. They turn to use alcohol to avoid dealing with stress at the workplace or home, while some turn to hard drugs to get quick relief from their stress.

However, this may work just for a temporary moment. Once the impacts of alcohol or drugs blur away, the individual will begin to feel the stress again. This is one of the smarter reasons to find permanent stress relief instead of using the escapism strategy way to deal with stress.

Irrational behavior is among the traits of a stressed person; some refer to it as "One not being themselves," they will make haste decisions that totally appear to be out of their character. The decisions they make may not be that terrible, they may appear acceptable in the real sense, but they may have negative repercussions about it.

A stressed person may start an argument over every minor issue due to irritability behavior. They may also seem to get frustrated over things that aren't serious. For example, a stressed dad may start yelling at his kids for making the slightest error, such as breaking the teacup. The stressed individual also tends to be quick-tempered; they are probably going to have a strong, passionate reaction to everything.

Attempting to make a joke or trick some stressed individuals can undoubtedly get you in a significant issue, some stressed individual likewise becomes brutal, they may get into physical battles with the slightest provocation whether genuine or perceived. Some even get into a fight even with little or no provocation.

Cognitive Effects

One of the most widely known psychological effects of stress is memory decline, meaning a stressed individual will easily forget things. They will make arrangements and totally disregard it; a stressed worker will overlook his task totally, while a stressed life partner will overlook significant dates, such as an anniversary. This forgetfulness might be short- or long-term.

Individuals tend to lapse in memory; they will be most likely to recollect things they say or did sometime in the past. This essentially occurs because of the inability of the minds to concentrate on anything else apart from the stressor.

This can greatly hinder a person's performance in many areas; a stressed worker will not be able to concentrate at work, and therefore they may end up losing their job. The stressed student will also be unable to concentrate on their academics and may begin performing inadequately. A stressed individual will also have a low sex drive; they will pull back from all forms of intimacy. Stress can undoubtedly destroy a relationship because of the absence of intimacy.

Positive Effects of Stress

The impacts of this stress are usually good; they can help an individual to be more creative or help in gaining the necessary energy and motivation to achieve a given task.

How to Block The Behaviors Keeping Your Stress Alive

There are three obsessive behaviors that you likely to be engaging in that obstructed your recuperating cycle and stopped you from enjoying a stress-free life. Recognizing these barriers can be a great initial move towards disposing of the issues that go with being too stressed.

The first is obsessive negativity. At the point of being obsessively negative, it implies that you have a tendency towards being "negative" about people, places, situations, and things throughout your life.

Maybe you always end up making statements like "I can't do this" or "nobody understands!" or "nothing ever works!" For instance, you might be doing this unconsciously, but essentially you have what's known as a "sour grape" mentality, and its keeps you away from realizing what it means to view life from a positive perceptive and appreciate the excellence in yourself and individual around you. There's an entire world out there for you with bliss and positive reasoning.

The second behavior you need to block is obsessive perfectionism; you are always centered on how to do everything right "just so" to the point of driving yourself into a restless condition. You may find yourself making expressions such as "I need to do this right!" or "I will be a failure!" or "if I am not precise, people will be mad at me."

Although this behavior may be totally under the threshold of your awareness, yet it will always interfere greatly with your ability to appreciate things life has to offers without feeling "uptight" or stressed."

The obsessive analysis is the final behavior you need to block when you are obsessed with analyzing things. You will always end up needing to re-hash an assignment or an issue over and over again.

You will always end up saying expressions such as "I have to look this over, study it, and know it inside and out or else I will not relax" or "if I relax and let things go without looking them more than once, things may turn out badly."

When analyzing, the reasoning is a great character; if it's done in excess, you will never get the chance to stop and smell the roses because you are too busy trying to figure out everything and everybody around you.

Gaining up knowledge of this kind of behavior is one of the most significant keys to relinquishing stress and getting total control over your anxiety. If you find yourself taking part in any of the above

"Blocking behavior," here are two things you can do to support yourself. Begin by asking the individuals you know, love, and trust, these questions. "Am I negative about things?" "Do I complain a lot?" and "Am I too difficult to be around?"

The answer you got might be difficult for you to listen to, as reality at times hurt a lot. But the understanding you will get from others' evaluation of you is priceless, and you will know precisely how others see you. Acknowledge their remarks as helpful info, and know that you will gain amazing insights from what you hear.

Second, keep a journal or diary to record and establish patterns of when you are utilizing "blocking behaviors." Even if you are not excited about the idea of writing, you can keep little entries in your notebook or journal each day.

The incredible part of this action is that you will start to see patterns in your behavior that reveal exactly what you are doing that are preventing you from getting your cure anxiety.

Chapter 3:
Stress and Your Self-Esteem

Stress and self-esteem are intricately linked in the same way that stress is linked to physical and mental health. Not only does low self-esteem make you more vulnerable to stress, but chronic stress of all kinds — physical, emotional, environmental, social, personal, and so on — can profoundly impact your self-esteem.

The Stress/Self-Esteem Cycle

Let's look at how stress can subtly undermine your self-esteem. It's often hard to pinpoint where the cycle begins. Imagine for a moment that you've had a very stressful day. (Maybe you don't have to imagine!) It seems like everything has gone wrong. You smacked your foot on the bottom step. You spilled coffee on your jacket on your way out the door. Your car wouldn't start. And then, at work, your boss dumped a project on you that will make the next two months extremely difficult. You envision many long nights ahead. You have to miss lunch. A colleague tells you that you "look terrible."

Then, when you get home at the end of the day, you scrap your plans to go to the gym; you order a pizza and eat the whole thing. Then, you feel guilty. You feel bad about skipping your exercise, about giving in to junk food, about eating way too much. You feel so guilty that you make yourself an ice cream sundae and stay up late watching TV. Forget the dishes.

In the morning, you wake up puffy and lacking energy. A messy kitchen greets you, you go to work exhausted, and you've got all the same stress you had the day before. So, the cycle continues. You keep overeating, under sleeping, and not doing anything about the things that are causing your stress, whatever they are. Maybe you don't have the energy, and maybe you have no idea what you could possibly do about it. Instead, you begin to feel worse and worse about yourself because you are so tired, so overwhelmed, and so unable to exercise your willpower. The worse you feel about yourself, the more you are likely to continue in the destructive pattern.

The stress cycle works in both directions. Stress can cause low self-esteem, but low self-esteem can be a major contributor to your stress level. If you don't feel good about yourself, lack confidence, or doubt your ability to succeed, you'll be more likely to let stress overwhelm you.

So, what are you supposed to do about this insidious cycle? Solutions are often difficult to come by, especially since the problems don't seem to begin anywhere in particular. How do you jump in and slam on the brakes? By jumping in and slamming on the brakes, that's how!

Build Self-Esteem by Demolishing Excess Stress

The first step in breaking the stress/self-esteem cycle is to isolate something you can do something about. It doesn't have to have anything to do with self-esteem. It's important to start with one thing since one of the characteristic conditions of stress is a lack of focus. If you have so many things going on in your life and you feel overwhelmed, you probably know what it is like to wander around in a daze, unable to do any of them. Maybe you do a little of one project but then get distracted by the pressing deadline of another, so you do a little of that one but once again are distracted by something else that needs attention. Before you know it, another day is gone, and nothing has been finished.

To repeat, the best way to take action to break the cycle is to choose one single thing you can do something about, something you can finish. Yes, lots of other things need finishing, but they aren't going to get finished anyway as long as you are feeling the way you are feeling. You know it's true! The only way to make a difference is to focus.

The way you choose to focus is up to you. It might require getting one thing accomplished on your to-do list — accomplished all the way. Or, it might involve some enforced personal time. Meditation might be what it takes to stop that horrible incessant buzzing in your head that is interfering with your productivity and making you feel so rotten about yourself.

What you choose to do also depends on the kind of stress overwhelming you. Let's look at some of your options for conquering stress in a way that, at the same time, specifically helps you to fortify your self-esteem. Let's also look at how each strategy might be used most effectively.

If you don't have a good (pleasant, safe) place to walk in your neighborhood or if the weather is rotten, have a walking backup plan, such as the track, the gym, or the mall. Although, as you know, exercise helps relieve stress, a reflection walk can help relieve stress and make you feel better about yourself at the same time.

This is what you do: first, put on comfortable walking shoes and comfortable clothes that will "work" for moderate exercise and also make you feel good about yourself. In other words, let your criteria be to dress so if you happen to meet someone you know, you won't feel self-conscious about what you are wearing. Brush or comb your hair. Wash your face, put on some sunscreen, and, if it makes you feel more human, put on some makeup. Go to the front door and take five deep, full breaths. Then, out loud, say: "I'm ready to reflect upon all the good things in my life."

Then, out the door, you go! Walk for thirty minutes at a moderate pace – just fast enough to feel as though you are getting some exercise but not enough to wear you out or make you frustrated or your muscles sore. As you walk, continue to take deep breaths and, most importantly, begin your mental list of all the things that are good about your life.

Here are some questions to consider:

• What is working?

• What parts of your life make you feel great?

• Who are the people in your life that make your life better?

• Whom do you love?

• What do you like about yourself?

• What are some of your fondest memories?

• Where do you love to go?

• What are your favorite things to do?

- What foods make you feel really good?

- What is your favorite book?

- What is it that you love about your home, your pets, your car, and your job?

- In what areas of your life are you successful?

Don't undermine your own efforts at building up your self-esteem by telling yourself that any accomplishment isn't worth celebrating. If you, say, finally balanced the checkbook, or vacuumed, or turned off the TV last night earlier than you normally would, that's great! Or, maybe you didn't eat that bag of cookies or spend that $50 on stuff you don't need. You can and should feel good about things like that!

You can get as general as "I love my kids" or as specific as "I set up a system for paying my bills on time that works really well." If you are having trouble focusing or thinking of things, set a goal, such as adding one item to your mental list for every twenty-five steps or for every five breaths. If you get stuck, stop until you think of something, then move on.

The challenge of the reflection walk is to put aside for the thirty minutes all the things that aren't working - the negativity, the things you think you should be doing. After the walk is over, get back to work but put all your stressful thoughts aside for now. They'll still be there when you get back, but they may not seem quite so overwhelming once you've put them in perspective. After a reflection walk, your life will probably look a lot better, and you'll feel a lot better about yourself, too.

Seeing Green

When it comes to natural beauty — meaning forests, mountains, flower gardens, and other such scenery — some people can take it or leave it. Other people find that being in or even just looking at natural beauty has a profound effect on how they feel about their lives, the world, and themselves. If you are interested in Ayurveda and have discovered that you are a Pitta type, you are probably one of these people. But even if you don't know anything about Ayurveda, you probably know whether natural beauty has a strong effect on you.

Even if you live in the city, you can use natural beauty to help you relieve stress and feel better about yourself. Surrounding yourselves with images of natural beauty can give you little lifts all day long. Here are some ways to accomplish this:

• Tonight, instead of your usual sitcoms or drama lineup, watch the Discovery Channel, Animal Planet, or a nature show on public television. It's good for your brain, food for your soul, and you just might learn something!

• Spend thirty minutes puttering around your own microenvironment. Even if your yard or the area around your apartment building is small, it probably contains some green stuff. Meander, examining each tree, flower, patch of grass, or plant bed. Don't think about anything else. Just see how much you can observe.

• Get to know the trees on your property. Some cultures believe the trees are spirit guardians. Look at and think about the trees surrounding your home. If the spirit moves you, you might even ask for their protection. Who knows?

• If you have no microenvironment on your property worth examining (although even a single flower can be worth examining), walk or drive somewhere close by, for example, a park or a nicely landscaped neighborhood. Walk around and look, look, look. Fill up your brain with natural beauty, and there won't be room for anxiety, at least not during that thirty minutes you've reserved for this purpose.

• Grow an herb garden or a small flower garden, either from seeds or by transplanting purchased plants in a large planter. Put the planter on your patio, deck, front step, or back step, or in a sunny window. Check and tend it daily. It's like taking vitamins for your soul!

• Go to your local library or bookstore and browse through a book that contains large color photographs of natural beauty. Maybe you'll feel transported by a photo essay on Hawaii, or maybe the Rocky Mountains are more your style. Or Europe? Africa? The Central American rain forests? Let your imagination whisk you away for thirty minutes.

• Plan your next vacation around a natural wonder, such as the Grand Canyon, or take a cruise to the Caribbean, or camp in a national park or forest, or go to a beach in a neighboring town. Okay, this takes more than thirty minutes, but not if you average it out over the year.

Do One Thing All the Way

This one's for all of you who feel like all the little things in your life are out of control. If you have so many things to do that you can't seem to finish any of them, take thirty minutes and complete just one of the short chores listed below. You'll get a feeling of accomplishment you could never get from half-finishing twenty different chores. None of these chores takes very long, but they are all things that a lot of people have a hard time getting around to. When they remain undone, they weigh on your mind and add to your stress and the sense that you aren't able to keep things under control.

Doing just one thing on this list each day can make a huge difference in how you feel about yourself. Try it for a week. You'll see.

• Clean out your car. Throw out all the trash, return the recyclables, put everything back in the house that belongs in the house, and attack those floor mats with the hand vac. Then, wipe down the windows with glass cleaner.

• Clean out your purse or wallet. Throw away all the junk you don't need. File the receipts and put everything in the right place. Flatten out your money and stack it so that all the bills face the right way. Clean out all the loose change and put it in a jar somewhere. (If you do this every day, you may soon have enough change in that jar to cover college tuition!)

• Spend some quality time with your pet. Pets relieve stress. And because they seem to love us unconditionally, they can make us feel pretty good about ourselves, too.

• Clean out the coat closet. Take out all the things that don't belong in there and put them away properly. Hang up all the coats that have fallen or have half fallen off the hangers. Store all the scarves, hats, mittens, and earmuffs in a bin. Give away all the stuff that doesn't fit anymore or that nobody wants. Wow! Who knew you had all that space in there?

• Balance your checkbook. Quit griping or dreading it. Just go do it.

• Call the dentist and make an appointment. And keep the appointment!

• Go to your desk and take one manageable stack from your many stacks of things that need to be filed or put away, and file or put away everything in that one pile.

• Drink a really big glass of water all the way. Finish the whole thing.

• Dust all the flat surfaces in your living room. This should take only five minutes, but it makes a perceptible difference.

• Make your bed. Just do it.

• Take a bath or a shower, then put moisturizer on every square inch of your skin. Put on a bathrobe and relax for fifteen minutes.

• Sweep the garage. Don't worry about the other stuff in there; just sweep out all the dirt you can get to.

• Remember that call you've meant to make to work out that problem with that company? Make the call.

• Groom, the dog. Just do it.

• You know that thing you've been meaning to tell that person but keep forgetting or putting off? Tell him.

• Set aside fifteen minutes — just fifteen minutes! — to start, experience, and finish your own personal time. Go to a quiet room after instructing others you are not to be disturbed, set a timer, and do something all on your own that you really want to do, and do it for fifteen minutes solid. Read, listen to music, sew, whittle, whistle, whatever. Don't gyp yourself. Do the whole fifteen minutes, start to finish. Voilà! You're ready to continue with your day.

• Take a water day. Don't drink anything but water all day long. Just for one day. (If you are addicted to caffeine, you might need just one cup of black coffee or tea in the morning to avoid the inevitable headache.) If you drink about eight cups of water during the day, you'll feel lighter, airier, and you'll have more energy.

Commit to Yourself

It's all well and good to manage your stress for the sake of the others in your life, but you have to commit to yourself, too. Self-esteem, at its very basic level, is about recognizing that you are worth self-care. And, of course, that means you'll be better able to care for others. As the Buddha once said, "Be a light unto yourself." Seek self-knowledge, treat yourself well, care for yourself, and you'll learn to love, appreciate, and esteem yourself.

Then, when stress happens, which it will, you'll understand that the stress that happens outside of you doesn't change who you are, what you are worth, how precious and individual and worthy of self-love you are.

No one understands you as you do, and if you don't try to understand yourself, you can't expect others to. So, make it a point to understand, study, nurture, and honor yourself. The rest — including all those things that cause the stress in your life — will fall right into place.

Chapter 4: *Motivate Your Groundbreaking Resolve to Dig Down to the Roots of Your Stressed Energy*

Groundbreaking solutions are always unconventional, novel, and bring up something hitherto unknown to exist. Thus, making a groundbreaking resolve is daring a miracle. However, there has to be a spark of knowledge that motives you to keep magnifying by feeding it with more mental energy, psychic energy, and more spiritual energy. The groundbreaking discovery of an oil well exemplifies this kind of scenario.

Layout a success foundation – in your mind!

Success is a state of mind. If you want success, start thinking of yourself as a success." – Joyce Brothers

Success is created in your mind as a MASTERPLAN. There's nothing you can create in the physical realm that wasn't already created in the mental realm. The 3D Vision is the architectural masterpiece of your master plan. It is the container within which your ultimate success will reside... once actualized.

Like establishing a building foundation, you have to clear obstacles such as tree stumps, big rocks, and such other obstacles so that you have a surface that you can work on. The same happens with laying out success foundation in your mind.

Overcome the obstacles that blocked your mind

The biggest wall you have to climb is the one you build in your mind: Never let your mind talk you out of your dreams, trick you into giving up. Never let your mind become the greatest obstacle to success. To get your mind on the right track, the rest will follow. – Roy T. Bennett

Just as the master plan rests in your mind, so are the obstacles. The most difficult obstacles to overcome aren't those in the physical realm but those in the mental realm. Such obstacles include:

· Negative attitude

· False assumptions (fallacies)

· Limiting beliefs

· Bad habits

· Destructive fears

· Repellant behaviors

To overcome these obstacles, you need to have the WILL to accept and the POWER to do. These two words join forces to form WILLPOWER. Thus, you need to work on your willpower!

Work on your willpower

The difference between a successful person and others is not a lack of strength, not a lack of knowledge, but rather a lack in will.
– Vince Lombardi

Willpower is the most omnipotent word when it comes to changing your mindset. It's the orbit that other methods and strategies revolve around and without which the center cannot hold.

Your willpower: the power of an indomitable persistence

Life is a gift. And it can only be awarded in the present. The power to award this gift is now, not in the past, and not in the future – but now. This power is your willpower. No other power can gift you with this present... neither from those whose existence your birth manifested nor from those whom you came into being that became your family and its associations – but you!

There's simply no power greater than your willpower. It's by sheer willpower that you can jailbreak from the traps of mental limitations that make you feel stressed up. And it's by sheer willpower that you can set your mind free.

Seize your willpower and ignite it to explode your inner exuberance. And like a volcanic eruption, let this exuberance meltdown all the rocks of obstacles within, thus creating pathways to your inner freedom. So, let the overflowing lava of this inner exuberance craft paths on the landscape of reality to your outer freedom. Let this rich lava pave your path to success.

Let your mind regain its control. Your mind was born free. And so, let it remain free. Strip it naked. Free it back to its nativity. All that you need to get started is to regain your willpower.

So, what is willpower?

Willpower is the most omnipotent word when it comes to changing your mindset. Willpower is a compound word that blends two important words, 'will' and 'power.' Thus, to comprehensively understand it, it's important to first digest what will is before digesting what willpower is.

The will is the yearning to make a conscious choice. It's manifested in the express desire to do something.

The power on the other hand refers to the ability to act. It's force of authority. It's the directed thrust of your energy channeled towards achieving your will. It's the ability to transform wealth into a need-satisfying purpose.

Important characteristics of willpower: many define willpower in limited terms – as the ability to control oneself. I consider control as just one element of willpower. In this regard, the following are some of the main characteristics of willpower:

· Being conscientious of your actions.

· Exerting self-control so that your energy is directed towards achieving your goals.

· Restraining impulsive and irrational urges that run contrary to your goals.

· Emotional control.

· Determination to achieve your goals.

· Self-igniting combustion of productive energy triggered by the will.

· Ability to focus and concentrate your energy on long-term goals and thus forgo instant gratification that could counter your set goals.

· The power to start the wealth-generating engine.

Why do you need willpower?

Willpower is the ignition key to the wealth generator. Without willpower, this wealth generator cannot start, leave alone run. And without this engine running, there's simply no success.

So, any moment when you feel poor ask yourself, where's the ignition key to my wealth generator? Has my wealth generator started? Is it running? This is a quick jumpstart into your diagnostic process.

When you get stressed, it means that your mind is struggling to turn over the ignition key. The wealth engine isn't igniting. And is this frustrated energy by the failure to jumpstart your wealth-generating engine that brings stress.

What breeds willpower?

Willpower is the product of you ingeniously programming your mindset such that the input that gets into your mind gets an output that propels you into positive action. This positive action is excited by the positive self-image that you manifest from the feedback of the processing function within your brain. It's like typing something on the keyboard and what you get on the screen makes you laugh, exclaim, and ooze confidence that you are ready to pursue your goals.

Sometimes, you may type the same thing, and depending on the mindset (how the mind is programmed or 'set'), you get some image or content that dampens your spirit or forces you to switch off the computer and wallow in the misery of negative thoughts. The difference between the two experiences is how you programmed your mindset.

The following are the important quality factors that boost willpower:

· Self-awareness

· Reflection

· Introspection

· Good health

These specifics practices can greatly improve these quality factors:

· Meditation

· Mindfulness

· Positive affirmations

· Power posing

· Creative visualization

· Yoga

How do you boost your willpower?

Your willpower is the engine that propels the execution of your wealth-generation strategy. To boost your willpower, you need to:

a. Learn and discover situations where you feel your choice is limited, inadequate, or hindered so that you can exert more force to overcome the obstacles.

b. Explore and find ways by which you can do that which you feel you're "compelled" to do but in a way that reinvigorates your will and strengthens your resolve. Remember, no outside force can compel you to do anything. It's your choice. It's your inner compulsion.

c. Put yourself in a situation where you have to make decisions and abide by them. You can begin with those decisions that you are not accountable to anyone, such as stopping sugar addiction, waking up early, stopping smoking, etc.

d. Once you build your confidence in standing by your small decisions, you can now move to make big decisions.

e. Comprehend the impact of lack of willpower on your life and its consequences. To achieve this, complete an internal audit of your past performance and imagine how different you would have performed if you had the willpower. Further, imagine how your desired state would be had you achieved your strategic outcomes.

f. Stop unwarranted procrastination and start taking action now. Kick out your inertia through a strong stroke of ignition. For example, if you're reluctant to get out of bed, let it be the moment that you jump out of it. If you're feeling such lazy to do fitness workouts, do instant press-ups. If you feel awful about apologizing to that person that you wronged, pick up the phone and call now. And if you feel lazy to chart out your plan, pick a pen and a paper and start laying it out now.

g. Visualize a whole new world of infinite possibilities available to you for years or even decades to come should you quit bad habits and embrace good habits that help you achieve your soul's grandest ideal.

h. Go beyond your comfort zone and start doing that which unsettles you but is the right thing to do. For example, if you feel you're now too old to study, it's time to enroll in a training program; if you're scared of that side-hustle, it's now time to start it. And if you've always felt like moving out of your current unpleasant neighborhood, it's now time to start packing as you seek out your desired neighborhood.

i. Dare to confront and accomplish challenges that come your way without fear.

j. Break down your tasks into small daily, hourly, or even minute goals that you can easily accomplish as you get on to accomplish more.

i. Target wholesome wellbeing by doing what works best for your overall good.

k. Do reward yourself in a manner that motives you and refuels your desire to achieve more.

By boosting your willpower, you can boost your wealth-generation potential. Your wealth-generating engine is eagerly waiting for that igniting stroke of willpower.

How to use life quotes to fire up the motivation you need to radically change your life?

Life quotes are the living words of people's experiences over time. Some quotes are as old as two thousand years and even more. Yet, they continue to nurture and guide us through our daily lives. They're our best heritage from our ancestors and the living sages. With them, we can avoid so many pitfalls that they identified and have an easier journey through life. Yet, more importantly, life quotes can radically change your life. How? You only need to know how to use them in the most impactful way.

We've already used some life quotes in this book, albeit sparingly. But, don't forget that all quotes are a product of the mind. You, too, have a mind, so don't lay to waste your ingenious power to teach the world through quotes.

Writing quotes, just like writing poetry, is a habit that you can easily build. Once you invite the habit, your subconscious mind feeds you with the raw materials... and the conscious mind beautifies them using its experience.

Writing quotes is a highly rewarding thing to do. It's also one of the best ways to anchor your mind to re-enact a certain experience. If the experience is motivating, innervating, energizing, and inspiring, that's a dose of joy and happiness.

Create your own list of life quotes

The best point to start from is to create a list of life quotes. There are books containing such lists. However, the best way is to write them down on your own. What you write down yourself sticks more than that which you simply read. You can write your own quotes by simply cultivating the habit of writing down your thoughts.

Narrate a brief story of your life encounters that validate the life quote

Every life quote is an encrypted code of a book of life. As such, it's heavily condensed. You need to de-condense it so that it becomes easily digestible to your mind and those you endeavor to share it with.

Reciting and regurgitating quotes cannot transform you. It cannot radically change your life. What can radically change your life is experiencing the quotes in a practical sense.

Have a brief story of your life around a given quote. This way, you'll remember it. You'll also be in a position to inspire others by narrating your story around the quote. It could as well be the start of your new career as a motivational speaker or counselor. Who knows?

Find a quote that's relevant to your current happening and relate to it.

Whenever something unique happens to your life, or simply something significant, attach a relevant quote to it. This quote could be the most powerful guide on what you ought to do next after the event.

Use life quotes to warn, encourage, advise, comfort, and inspire others

The wise, the sages, and the noble of yesterday weren't rich (in material terms). They never commanded armies. Yet, they were looked upon due to their ability to inspire communities, societies, and nations through wise words. It's their wise words that we quote. Don't just give a plain warning. The package is wrapped in a life quote that makes someone think twice.

Don't just encourage using plain words. Add in life quotes that comfort and inspire. They're the kind of seasoning that makes the food of life delicious. Don't just advise using technical jargon. Instead, use life quotes that bring deeper insight and reflection. It's merely a matter of having a bigger impact on the heart than on the brain.

By doing this and making this your habit, you will not only have transformed others but also have radically changed your life.

Create a group where you can discuss one life quote a day or one life quote a week.

It's commonly said two heads are better than one. I'd also said that two hearts are better than one. Being together to share a quote and narrate your life experiences can be greatly uplifting. You not only empower others with a new narrative but you also get empowered by a new narrative from each one of them. This is the power of the multiplier effect.

You radically get transformed by this multiplier effect, which would not have happened had you just been alone sharing your narrative with no one else.

Relate your future plans with your life quote by creating a calendar of life quotes – remember to have a quote for each item on your To-Do list!

If there's anything that can empower you to actualize your dreams, nothing does it better than powerful, relevant, and inspiring life quotes. They always stick around. They always ring. They're the untiring reminders that you need to wake up to fulfill your dreams.

One of the best ways to let life quotes guide your future plans is to have a calendar of events in your plans being embellished by life quotes. Also, create a To-Do list with the last line of an item being reserved for one relevant life quote. This way, you will be inspired to accomplish the task. Furthermore, it could shape your perspective on how you go about doing it.

Keep cultivating your list of quotes

This is your garden. Plow it. Weed it. Fertilize it... and do all the tending. The harvest is all for you. Add more quotes, and remove those that no longer inspire. Only keep that which is worth it. Keep visiting the store for more planting seeds for your next season.

Chapter 5: *Approaching the Exercises*

You'll have lots of exercises to choose from that you can use on a daily basis to manage the stress in your life. In addition, write-on lines accompanying the exercises will help you record your experiences, your physical, emotional, psychological, and behavioral responses, and how you decide to change them to make your life healthier and happier.

First, use this checklist to clarify where you are in terms of life changes. Use the blanks next to the checkboxes at the bottom of the list to add any major life changes not covered here, and check those off as well.

Major Life Change Checklist

In the last year . . .

☐ I started a new relationship

☐ I ended a relationship

☐ I got married

☐ I got separated

☐ I got divorced

☐ I welcomed a child into my family

☐ I lost a child

☐ I lost a parent

☐ I lost a close friend or family member

☐ I was diagnosed with a chronic or severe illness

☐ My partner, child, or parent was diagnosed with a chronic or severe illness

☐ I moved to a new home

☐ I moved to a new city

☐ I started a new job

☐ I was fired or laid off from a job

☐ I started a business

☐ I closed a business

☐ My partner lost a job

☐ My partner lost a parent

☐ My partner lost a close friend or family member

☐ I started school.

☐ I had legal problems

☐________________________________

☐________________________________

☐________________________________

Set the Stage

Before you start doing the exercises, you need to be in the right frame of mind. You need to be optimistic about the possibilities for changing your life in the future, open to the experience of learning something new, and willing to risk failure while remaining excited about the possibility of success.

Sometimes all you will need is one minute to catch your breath and slow yourself down. But other times, you may need to disengage from your work routine, get out of the office, and engage in a 10-minute activity. Your choice of exercises may be constrained by your location or how much time you have to do an exercise. For example, if you are getting stressed in a business meeting, you may not be able to take a 10-minute time-out to get yourself together, but a one-minute breathing or visualization exercise while taking a trip to the bathroom may be all you need to get you back to the best of who you are.

To set the stage for the exercises, you need to be aware of what you are feeling and thinking. If you are not conscious of the stress you are feeling, you will not be able to make the choice that is right for you. This requires you to be fully present in the moment.

Here's how to work through the exercises, from start to finish:

1. Decide what you will use for a timer. This could be your watch, your phone, or the clock on the wall. In situations where using a timer may not be practical, like in a meeting where you don't want to be seen watching the clock or checking your phone, or where an alarm will disturb others, you can still do the exercises while simply estimating the time. Not all exercises in the book require using a timer anyway, as simply following the instructions will take about one, five, or 10 minutes.

2. If you can, remove yourself from the physical location of the source of your stress.

3. Close your eyes and take one deep breath. Open your eyes.

4. Follow the directions of the exercise.

5. Lastly, record in the margins of this workbook which exercise you chose, the date, time, and location of when you did the exercise, and whether the exercise worked. Depending on where you are, you may not have access to this book; if you don't, use a note-taking app on your cell phone to record your activity and later copy your results here.

State Your Goals

Now that you know how stress impacts your life, use that information to determine your goals with the exercises. Yes, you want to reduce your overall stress level, but what else do you want to accomplish with these exercises?

Perhaps you want to reduce a particular stressor, react differently to a particular trigger, or be able to re-center yourself when you are beginning to feel overwhelmed. You may want to start the day in a calmer frame of mind or be able to calm yourself in the evening to enjoy a longer, deeper sleep that leaves you feeling rested and alert.

Maybe your goal is to become a master of peace and tranquility, be less stressed at work, or be less distracted by stress and more present when you're with your family and friends. Thinking about your goals now will make choosing your exercises easier and help you make more appropriate choices.

When do you want to do your stress management exercises? Think about whether you want a schedule of little breaks throughout the day and if you want to use them in the morning to start your day in the right mood, or whether you will rely on them to help you relax and sleep better at night. Feel free to combine all these options and add your own, but try not to schedule more exercises than you think you will actually engage in. You can always start in the area(s) of most urgent need and gradually expand your exercise practice to other areas of your life.

Where do you plan to do your stress management exercises? Will you be at work, at home, on the road, or a combination of all of the above? This will determine the kind of exercises you do. For example, it will be easier to do dancing and stretching exercises at home because your office situation may not be conducive to that kind of activity. You may not want to access YouTube or travel websites at the office since you don't want your boss thinking that you're not focused on your job. Some exercises are hard to do on a plane or while driving and may not be suitable for managing your stress while in transit.

Choose Your Exercises

How will you decide which exercises are right for you, given the goals you have articulated and how you want to incorporate the stress management exercises into your life? Let's start with how much time you have to dedicate to your self-care process. This workbook shouldn't be one more thing you have to do that may cause you even more stress. Only you know how much time you have to take care of yourself.

But note that because stress can get in the way of your performance, completing the exercises will improve your performance and give you more quality time in your busy day. Of course, the more time you have to dedicate to your stress management practice, the better you will feel. That said, you'll begin to feel changes with just a few one-minute exercises per day. Many of the exercises lend themselves to being repeated throughout the day, so, if possible, try to schedule breaks all day long. If you can't, using the exercises in the morning and/or evening will reduce stress as well.

If you want to calm yourself down, breathing exercises will be very helpful. If you are feeling muscle tension, you will want to do a stretching exercise. And if you want to prepare for a stressful event, you may want to do a visualization exercise that helps you reorient your thinking to focus on success.

Your Physical Needs

Physical self-care involves caring for your body in ways that sustain, revitalize, and strengthen it. When we do not take care of our bodies, we take the risk of becoming sick or not being able to move around as quickly and painlessly as we would like. Physical self-care gives our body the strength it needs to help us do the things we sometimes take for granted, like walk, run, swim, and dance. Physical self-care involves three components: physical movement, sleep and rest, and proper nutrition.

The physical movement carries a number of health benefits, including promoting improved brain functioning, enhanced sleep quality, and reduced risk of illness and disease. Doctors recommend that adults get two and a half to five hours per week of moderate-intensity exercise that gets their hearts pumping. Light bicycling, swimming, walking briskly, gardening, running, boxing, hiking, jogging, and playing a team sport, like basketball are just a few exercises we can do for our cardiovascular health. In addition, we can keep ourselves physically strong by engaging in strength-training activities (such as lifting free weights or using weight machines), as well as body weight exercises (such as push-ups) and sports, like rock climbing.

We get the most benefit from physical activity when we do it consistently and gradually challenge ourselves to reach the next level of intensity over time. Safety is also key! To prevent pain and possible injury, it's important to listen to your body and incorporate time for rest and recovery into your fitness routine.

Like exercise, sleep is extremely important for our day-to-day functioning. Adequate, regular sleep improves overall health and wellness by ensuring that we are functioning to the best of our ability—

physically, mentally, and emotionally. To be at our best, doctors recommend that, as adults, we get seven to nine hours of sleep. I know many of us are functioning on far fewer hours than we need for some very legitimate reasons. At the same time, our goal should always be to consistently reach a minimum of seven hours. How well we sleep is just as important as the number of hours we spend in bed. Both quantity and quality are important.

Eating a healthy diet means getting proper nutrients and calories from the foods and beverages we eat. Poor eating habits and an inadequate diet have been linked to obesity and the development of preventable chronic conditions such as diabetes and cardiovascular disease. Foods and beverages that fuel our bodies the best include a range of vegetables, whole fruits, whole grains, low- or fat-free dairy, a variety of proteins, and water. For optimal health and wellness, calories from artificial sugars, saturated fats, and sodium should be limited, and calories from nutrient-rich foods and beverages should be maximized.

Physical self-care also includes the way we think and feel about our bodies. This is known as our body image. It includes what you say to yourself when you look in the mirror and how you perceive yourself with regard to physical attributes, body weight, shape, and height, and your sense of your ability to influence and change your body. People with a positive body image focus more on their physical abilities and feel comfortable and confident about their bodies no matter how the physical appearance of their bodies may change over time. A positive body image can support your physical self-care by helping you accept yourself and your body even though you may be taking steps to improve your physical health.

One way to improve your body image is to focus on a goal other than changing your body. Why? Well, from a very young age, family members and peers give us feedback about our body weight. Much of this feedback is laced with negative judgments and comparisons that leave us feeling ashamed. On top of that, we are bombarded with messages from the media about how our bodies should look. As you begin your journey toward enhanced physical self-care, I encourage you to change this narrative. Resist the urge to internalize negative messages and focus instead on being grateful for the body you have and all it allows you to do.

Your Physical Self-Care Values

Here's an exercise to help you clarify your physical self-care values. Remember, values are like a life compass. They help guide your actions and motivate you to create meaningful habits. Get your notebook and answer the following questions.

•Imagine that you live in a society where, as an incentive for physical self-care, each adult is given two hours a day to focus solely on their physical self-care each and every day. You can work on your physical health in any environment you'd like and in any way you like. What would you do?

•There are a variety of ways you can improve your physical self-care during your daily two-hour time block, but imagine that you could select only ten activities from the following list. (Don't worry: After 12 months have passed, you can switch it up.) In your notebook, write down the ten activities you selected and rank them on a scale of 1 to 10, where 1 is the most important activity, and 10 is the least important activity. Keep in mind that you can do more than one of your selected activities during the two-hour period. For example, you could take a one-hour nap, do 30 minutes of cardiovascular exercise, and eat a mindful meal. There are no right or wrong answers.

•For each item on your list, evaluate why you chose that particular activity. Why does it matter to you? In what way will that activity help enhance your physical self-care? Why is it important to you to enhance your physical self-care in this manner? For each activity, you selected, complete the following sentence in your notebook: this item is important to me because . . .

Physical Self-Care Activities

- Cardiovascular fitness class (group or one-on-one)
- Coaching class or independent study on being kind and compassionate toward yourself when your actions are not in line with your physical self-care values
- Coaching class or independent study on developing a healthy body image
- Coaching class or independent study on how to eat in moderation and how to avoid overeating
- Coaching class or independent study on how to incorporate flexibility and balance into your eating habits and exercise routine
- Coaching class or independent study on how to unlearn unhelpful beliefs and attitudes about physical self-care
- Coaching class or independent study on improving sleep quantity and/or quality

- Coaching class or independent study on improving your health without shaming or punishing yourself
- Coaching class or independent study on maintaining a healthy physical self-care routine while traveling and during holidays and vacations
- Cooking class focused on a variety of healthy meals
- Cooking class focused on flavorful, healthy meals
- Cooking class focused on quick healthy meals
- Cooking healthy meals on your own
- Dance class (type of dance is up to you!) (group or one-on-one)
- Eat a healthy meal together as a family
- Eat a mindful meal
- Engage in a healthy bedtime routine
- Engage in physical movement as a family, such as a family bike ride or walk
- Fitness class focused on improving flexibility and core strength (group or one-on-one)
- Martial arts class (group or one-on-one)
- Nutrition class on changing unhealthy eating habits and improving your health without dieting
- Nutrition class on the main food groups
- Personal training session
- Practice making healthy choices at restaurants and social gatherings
- Strength-training class (group or one-on-one)
- Water exercise class or swimming

- Yoga class (group or one-on-one)

Obviously, we don't live in a society that requires us to engage in two hours of physical self-care daily. But imagining yourself in this scenario probably gave you a good idea of which type of physical activities you value. Knowing this can be the motivation you need to start taking action on your physical self-care.

Time to Engage

One thing that makes physical self-care so hard is that there is no one-size-fits-all approach. Each person has their own optimal physical health, body size, and food preferences. There is no finish line. Physical self-care is something we will work toward until our time on Earth is up. Another challenge related to physical self-care is that our busy schedules do not seem to allow for choosing whole and healthy foods, adequate sleep, and regular exercise.

Create a Physical Self-Care Schedule

Each week, perhaps on Sunday, before the workweek begins, spend some time planning how you'll do some physical self-care in the coming week. If you use a physical calendar, write in "physical self-care" on the days you selected. Pick the time, length, and frequency (throughout the week) that works best for you. If you use an electronic calendar, set the alarm to signal you that it is time for physical self-care. Protect this time as though it were an important appointment—because it is! Aside from an emergency, don't let anything get in the way of your scheduled physical self-care. If you must skip a session because something serious comes up, be sure to reschedule it.

During your physical self-care time, use the entire allotted time for your chosen activity. Minimize all distractions—for example, log out of your e-mail account and social media sites, silence your phone, close your door, make sure your kids are occupied or supervised, politely ask to be uninterrupted by those around you, and turn off the television.

Chapter 6: *Mindfulness*

Meditation: The Foundation of Mindfulness

Whether you are new to meditation or have been practicing for some time, it can be challenging to find the time or motivation to engage in formal practice. If you are currently feeling stressed out, which is highly likely considering you picked up this book, it probably feels overwhelming to add one more item to your already overflowing to-do list. How will you find time each and every day? I can completely understand this struggle.

Typically, when someone is feeling overextended, self-care practices are the first to go. It's much easier to sacrifice something for yourself rather than letting down the people around you. The truth is that showing up for yourself is not optional: it's necessary to create a sustainable lifestyle over the long run. Luckily, you only need about 10 minutes per day to receive the anxiety- and stress-reducing benefits of meditation. By carving out 10 minutes to sit quietly and focus on your breath, you can actually create more capacity to tackle your responsibilities and engage with your busy life.

The idea of finding time for yourself to sit quietly and reflect might sometimes sound very inviting. There are times when I feel particularly introspective and can spend hours in my bubble doing yoga, meditating, and journaling. Everyone oscillates between excitement and resistance. Whether you can dedicate 10 minutes or an hour per day, start where you are because a little goes a long way.

In the MBSR program at the Center for Mindfulness at the University of Massachusetts, participants practice six days per week. When they are forming a new habit, repetition is most important. Studies show that missing a session doesn't impact the habit formation process as long as consistency is present overall (Lally et al., 2009). Practicing daily helps create an automatic response, so you'll start to show up without much effort after about two months or sooner for some people (Lally et al., 2009). Imagine incorporating just 10 minutes of seated meditation into your morning or bedtime routine. After a while, you'll show up on your meditation cushion because it's just part of your routine, like brushing your teeth.

On paper, this may sound simple, but in reality, it may feel difficult to know exactly how to get started or when to practice. Generally, meditating in the morning is a great way to set a calm and focused tone for the day, plus all your activities and interactions won't be filling your quiet space. If you are a morning person, have a flexible schedule, or don't have little ones to tend to as soon as you wake up, by all means, practice in the morning.

However, if your mornings are too full or you're nocturnal like me, the early practice may not align with your natural rhythm or schedule. You can meditate anytime and still receive the benefits. It may just take a bit more time for the sediment to settle, for your body and mind to transition from busy to still. This process can feel uncomfortable at first, as it's hard to be with your thoughts, feelings, and sensations—that's why our lives are often so full of distractions.

The most difficult, but probably the most helpful, time to practice is during or after a stressful event. When I come home after an emotional day of seeing my psychotherapy clients, sometimes I just want to eat some comfort food and watch a movie. What this usually does is distract me from the difficult feelings instead of allowing me to work through them. When I choose to do some stretching on my yoga mat, spend a few minutes checking in with my breath, and journal about what I'm feeling, I can set the stress of my day down instead of allowing it to hang out in the background of my mind, waiting for me to go to sleep. Remember that practicing mindfulness helps calm those ruminating thoughts that nag at you after a stressful day. The following meditations will help you get started.

Mindful Morning Meditation

Meditation doesn't always have to happen sitting on the cushion. Meet yourself where you are to start your day off mindfully with this simple morning check-in.

1. When you wake up in the morning, take a moment to pause before you look at your phone or hop out of bed to get your coffee.

2. Keeping your eyes closed, notice your body lying on the bed, feeling the support of the bed underneath you and the weight of the blankets around you.

3. Feel your breath moving in and out, feeling your belly rise and fall on each breath.

4. Take a moment to set an intention for the day. How do you want to feel today? What actions will help you feel that way?

5. When you're ready, allow your eyes to slowly adjust to being awake and take in your surroundings before starting your day.

Meditation for a Stressful Day

This is meditation for those days that leave you feeling depleted and overstimulated. For added benefit, practice this meditation under a weighted blanket, with a heating pad, or while taking an Epsom salt bath. After the meditation, be gentle with yourself for the rest of the evening. Have a cup of herbal tea or get into bed early.

1. Find any comfortable position and bring your eyes to a close or low gaze (looking down into your lap).

2. Without placing any judgment, take a moment to notice the pace and quality of your breath. Is it fast, shallow, or labored? Just be aware of the state of your breath as it moves in and out.

3. Bring awareness to your physical body. Where do you feel tension, heaviness, pain, or numbness? As you breathe in, imagine sending cleansing, nourishing energy to those parts. As you breathe out, imagine softening and releasing whatever you are holding on to at this moment. Continue to breathe, and if it feels right, add a big audible sigh on the exhale.

4. Notice if your body wants to move or stretch in any way, and perhaps roll the neck from side to side, twist the torso, or bring the knees up to the chest and give yourself a hug.

5. Continue breathing and stretching for a few more minutes, then slowly bring your body back to stillness and open your eyes.

Learning the Role of Impartial Observer

Taking the stance of the observer allows you to be more present in your life as it unfolds. You begin to witness instead of critique. Remember that the goal is not to eliminate judgmental thinking altogether, as your brain is wired to assess and scan. The goal is to unhook from this tendency to see your experiences more clearly and with less bias.

Judgment is common to all humans: it's a tool we use to understand our complicated world. The problem is that judgments can become absolutes and create limitations. Ever notice that as soon as your inner critic shows up, your confidence melts away? Or you make an assumption about someone and realize later you were completely wrong? I've definitely been there and have almost missed out on important friendships, job opportunities, and feeling confident in myself. It's natural to fill in the details with assumptions when you don't have the whole story, but you want to make sure those assumptions don't become obstacles.

Let's look more closely at how judgments can play out in your life. Comparing yourself with others is so common, especially on social media. When you see someone's "highlight reel" online, miss out on a promotion at work, or have an argument, you may quickly jump to that shame-filled place of "I'm bad" or "I'm not good enough." There is this assumption that you are only valuable if your life is perfect or you're happy all the time, but this is absolutely not true or even attainable. You're just a human doing the best you can with what you have. Mindfulness helps you have more compassion for yourself and let go of the pressure to be perfect.

Another area of your life where judgment plays a starring role is in your interactions with others. Often a detail about someone triggers a feeling in you, causing you to make a judgment about them, either positive or negative. Perhaps their tone of voice reminds you of your loving grandmother, and you feel soothed, or their lack of boundaries reminds you of a manipulative ex-partner, and you can't get away fast enough. You think you know the whole story, but you are really taking a template in your mind and applying it blindly to this new person. This is why mindfulness is so important: it helps you calm your emotions and detach from your assumptions to see your current reality more clearly.

Self-judgment and judgment of others show up in so many areas. You can judge your thoughts, behaviors, emotions, physical appearance, success, productivity, status—you can even judge how good you are at meditating. Early in college, I had a friend who was very spiritual, and I would often compare myself to her. I judged the beginning of my mindfulness journey as inferior to where she was years into her practice. This became a big obstacle to finding my own way and led me to instead follow someone else's path. Taking a nonjudgmental stance helps you take in the full picture of your own experience instead of comparing it to someone else's. In the process, you can slow down the flood of emotions, soften your inner critic, and lower your stress reactivity.

You can also take the observer approach from your meditation practice out into the world. To get an idea of what that might look like, imagine you're at the beach on a crisp autumn day. There's no one there but you, the waves are calm, and the sky is clear with a few clouds. You relax on a blanket with your hands folded behind your head and watch the clouds slowly float by. At this moment, you are quiet as you note the quality and shape of the clouds. There is no critique or comparison, just being present to what you see around you. This is the observer in action, noticing and witnessing without any critique.

Instead of placing a value on your experiences, interactions, or self-worth, the observer just names the facts. In the exercises that follow, you will practice reflecting on your day and social interactions without judgment.

The Key To Well-Being

Your body holds a lot of wisdom and often gives you clues about your needs and emotional experiences. Think of a time when you had butterflies in your stomach from anxiety, heartburn after a stressful day, or a gut feeling about someone you just met for the first time. Even looking at the phrases we use to describe these common manifestations of emotional experience is telling.

According to the American Psychological Association, research is showing more and more proof that the gut can influence "emotional behavior, pain perception and how the stress system responds" (Carpenter, 2012). This brain-gut connection goes two ways, as the brain can also impact gut health. For instance, even mild stress levels can cause digestive health issues and decrease immune functioning (Carpenter, 2012).

There is a clear mind-body connection that you can tap into to learn more about yourself and your needs at any given moment. When I am stressed, I unconsciously hunch my shoulders or tense my feet. When I find myself in these postures, I know it's time to slow down, take a few breaths, and check-in with myself.

Paying attention to your body, thoughts, and emotional landscape can feel overwhelming or scary, especially if you have been focusing outward or have experienced trauma in the past. There are many reasons you may become uncomfortable looking within yourself and connecting to your body. Perhaps you're struggling to meet the expectations of society to look a certain way or have had some type of physical or emotional trauma. For the first 18 years of my life, I learned to disavow my emotions because my feelings were overwhelming. It wasn't until I had the opportunity to heal through psychotherapy and my mindfulness practice that I began to reunite with myself. I discovered a deep well of intuition and guidance that I'd never had access to before. Be patient with yourself, and give yourself time for your frozen awareness to thaw.

The Body Scan Meditation is the foundation of getting reacquainted with your thoughts, feelings, and physical sensations, but there are many opportunities to check in with yourself every day. The next two exercises will help you bring mind-body awareness to ordinary activities, such as taking a shower or preparing a meal. Feel free to apply this same conscious mindset to any activity throughout your day.

1. Listening to Your Body's Wisdom

Take a few moments to reflect on some of the ways your body expresses emotions or gives you clues about your needs. Include both positive and negative experiences.

2. Mindful Shower

The shower is often the one space completely without distractions. It's where you process your day, imagine past and future conversations, and come up with your best ideas.

3. Mindful Cooking

Applying your mindfulness practice to cooking is a great opportunity to slow down and engage the senses. For this exercise, prepare a simple meal, such as oatmeal or soup.

Creating A Relationship With Yourself

Self-inquiry is a process of exploring your inner world, reflecting on your experiences, and processing your emotions. I like to think of it as creating a relationship with yourself—mind, body, and spirit.

Some of the benefits of practicing self-inquiry and being more self-aware include:

- ▶ Living in accordance with your personal values
- ▶ Understanding your needs
- ▶ Setting the right goals for yourself
- ▶ Knowing when you need to set limits
- ▶ Creating more awareness of your thoughts, emotions, and sensations
- ▶ Processing your experiences
- ▶ Reducing stress levels
- ▶ Deepening self-compassion and emotional regulation
- ▶ Listening to your intuition and inner wisdom

Think about any other benefits of self-inquiry you have experienced in the past or hope to tap into going forward. Would you add anything to this list?

How do you cultivate self-inquiry in your daily life? Modern life has made it increasingly difficult to get quiet and listen to the subtle voice within. Because of this, the most effective way to nourish your self-inquiry practice is to schedule time for yourself. If you have already incorporated meditation into your routine, you can include your self-inquiry practice then. If not, set aside time during some part of your day to get quiet and engage in the practices listed here. Choose an item from your to-do list that you could delegate or delete, and think about how you can commit to making this time for yourself.

Personally, I engage in structured self-inquiry before bed by journaling about my day. I allow whatever comes to mind to flow onto the page without judgment. This allows me to reflect on my day in a structured way and notice what emotions have surfaced as a result. It can also be helpful to journal in the morning, allowing you to process and clear away material from your dreams, worries about your day, or other thoughts.

What types of self-inquiry call to you?

JOURNALING: Write down your thoughts and feelings.

DAYDREAMING: Allow your imagination to wander.

WRITING: Channel your experiences into a story or draft a letter to yourself.

SEATED MEDITATION: Sit quietly with your thoughts, emotions, and physical sensations.

ART: Make a collage or create a vision board.

MOVEMENT: Connect with yourself through dance, walking, or yoga.

TAROT CARDS: Use the cards as a guide.

PSYCHOTHERAPY: Enlist the help of an impartial other.

SELF-TALK: Have a verbal dialogue with yourself.

Self-inquiry will occur naturally during your mindfulness practices but can be deepened with more intentional self-reflection. The next two exercises will help you start to engage in self-inquiry throughout your day. Experiment with different practices to see what helps you get more in touch with your thoughts and feelings.

Building Your Mindfulness Muscle

You wouldn't expect an athlete who skips practices or training sessions to perform their best during a game. More likely, they would lag behind and be out of sync with their teammates. Think of mindfulness as practice and your life as the game. Although we don't always want to show up, practice prepares us to handle the pressure and stress of our lives.

Remember that it's less important how you practice mindfulness compared to how much you show up. It's okay to build slowly and be imperfect. If you miss a day or have less time to practice, don't let that stop you.

The first step in creating your mindfulness routine is thinking about how much time you plan to dedicate to your practice. Do you have time to dedicate 15 to 20 minutes per day? Excellent! Do you have closer to five minutes? That's great, too: start there. Whatever time you find to dedicate to your mindfulness routine, you will have to prioritize your needs and create space for your own wellbeing.

For some, this practice of self-care might feel edgy or guilt-inducing. It may be hard to say no to others, set boundaries around your time, or ask for help so you can take care of yourself. Brainstorm a few ways you can get your needs met, such as asking for help with childcare, reducing commitments at work, or being less available by phone in the evenings for friends.

Chapter 7:
Overcoming Stress

Emotions are healthy and an important piece of our coping and response apparatus. Difficult emotions occur when there is danger or something to be afraid of. Sadness occurs in response to a loss, and anger in response to frustration. When not acknowledged and handled the right way, these responses create stress, and stress affects emotions.

In today's society, most people are not taught how to deal with their emotions and end up being afraid of them. If someone is angry, it feels dangerous. If you are angry, you might feel unsafe. If you are envious, you will feel unhappy without any positive outcome.

If you grew up in an emotional household, you probably know what you are feeling. If you grew up in a home where emotions were frowned upon or not allowed, you might not know what they are. This exercise is designed to help you identify your emotions. The range of emotions is happiness, sadness, fear, and anger. Happiness feels good. Fear, anger, and sadness don't feel so good. To identify emotions when you are not used to them, you need to connect a situation with the way you felt inside. Identifying the physical cues to your emotions is a powerful way to know what you are feeling and will help you have more control over how you respond. Once you become aware of your emotions and realize that they are safe, you will find that they can be a great asset.

When you have difficult emotions such as anger, fear, and anxiety, you may not want to face them because they are uncomfortable. After you identify them, it is important to acknowledge them in a nonjudgmental manner. It is normal to feel emotions. They are a vibrant part of being alive. When you don't allow yourself to feel your emotions, they often translate into a physical problem such as high blood pressure, headaches, or muscular tension.

Watch, don't judge. When you have uncomfortable or difficult feelings, it is natural to want to avoid facing them. Often, we are trained to ignore them. "Don't cry," "Don't be angry," "Don't feel sad," "Don't be weak." Although commonly heard, these phrases create a problem because having feelings is a normal part of being human.

Another reason you may not want to feel a bad feeling is you think you need to do something in response to the feeling. However, feeling angry does not mean you have to beat someone up. Feeling sad does not mean you have to stay at home and disappear from the world.

Understanding Emotions

Human emotions have remained the same throughout evolution and are connected to complex physical responses to situations. When you are afraid or angry, your body produces a range of hormones, including adrenaline and noradrenaline. These activate the body's ability to escape or stay safe from an attack.

Unbottle Your Emotions

The human is a complex being. If you look at other species in the animal kingdom, you do not see them denying difficult feelings, suppressing them, or doing anything other than feeling them and expressing them. If you try to take a bone away while a dog is chewing on it, even the gentlest dog might bare his teeth and growl aggressively and, if you go further, bite you. That dog is angry and has no inhibition about expressing it. On the other hand, if you are uncomfortable with anger and someone does something that makes you angry, you might not acknowledge it; you might just bite your tongue and say nothing. Then, you might go home with a terrible headache and be unable to sleep; your blood pressure would go up, and you would spend the next four weeks ruminating about what you wish you had said. To express emotions, you can speak to another person, or if that is not possible because of your comfort level, you can express how you feel to yourself.

Acts of Kindness—to Yourself

In addition to the mindfulness methods you have learned to avoid or relieve stress, I want to address one more thing you can do to take care of yourself despite the hectic life you lead and all the responsibilities you have, you can soften your life. Today's world is very hectic, fast-paced and success driven. You most likely are running at top speed from the time you wake until you go to sleep. You also probably do not reserve time when you can simply physically stop. When the stress continues, however, you stay on high alert, and that can create physical and psychological problems.

You can counter those effects by being kind to yourself during the day. You can schedule the five-minute miracle by taking five-minute breaks between running from one errand to another or from one meeting to another. You can stop to have a coffee and smell the aroma. You can get yourself a treat. Think of two small luxuries you can give yourself every day. We hardly ever examine our schedule to see how it can be broken up. We tend to just ram through the day rather than plan it with time for ourselves built-in. Think about how you can make your day a friendlier and kinder one.

Getting Grounded

Grounding essentially means getting in touch with reality when your mind is taking off. It is the ability to detach from overwhelming feelings and be fully present during the immediate moment. If you are someone who experiences anxiety on a regular basis, there might be times when your anxiety overpowers your rational thought. If you were a victim of previous trauma, as in PTSD, for example, it could come flooding back with flashbacks or intense memories.

Drug cravings or self-harm impulses can also make you feel like you have no control. When this happens, your mind takes over your sense of reality. You may not be able to see a more realistic picture, and anxiety controls your reason. This can be very scary, and you must connect to reality as soon as you can. The most fundamental way to do this is to touch something real.

Handling the Tornado

In some instances, you may have difficulty controlling your emotions. You may have temper outbursts that create disturbances and get you in trouble. You may feel that you have no control over your anxiety. When your emotions are out of control, you probably feel helpless and unable to change your responses, which may be disruptive or inappropriate.

The major key to overcoming stressful emotions is to see when they are happening before the progression of a strong emotion is a trigger. When you start experiencing the physical signs of emotion, identify what emotion you are feeling. By identifying the emotion first instead of reacting to it, you can interpret the meaning of the situation to which you are reacting. Finally, you can react in a responsive and thoughtful manner. In order to remain not controlled by the emotion, you can intervene at any of these three points. The process of identifying the emotion gives you time before you react. You can then adjust your behavior accordingly.

Mindfulness Explained

It is important to understand that mindfulness is not the same as psychotherapy. Mindfulness teaches you how to detach from the thoughts that create stress. Cognitive therapy gives you the tools to defeat the thoughts that create stress. Cognitive therapy was developed by Dr. Aaron Beck in the late 1960s. In 1980, Dr. David Burns expanded the approach and wrote Feeling Good, the New Mood Therapy.

Let It All Out

Studies show that holding in your angry feelings can have detrimental effects on both your physical and mental health. Repressed or suppressed stress and anger are associated with higher rates of depression as well as physical problems such as high blood pressure, headaches, and stomach problems.

In this exercise, I'll guide you through a healthy practice of expressing your emotions. There are several methods to letting out your aggressive feelings. You can identify them and express them by screaming or hitting something harmless. You can identify them and visualize them blowing up and being pulverized. Lastly, you can identify them, notice that they are angry feelings, and let them float away. Whichever you choose, remember to do what feels comfortable.

Creating Positivity

Feeling positive has a component of doing things that are upbeat. It also is controlled by how you look at a situation, which affects how you feel. Very often, people find the negative in a situation rather than the positive, seeing the glass half empty. There are reasons for this, such as not getting your hopes up to avoid later disappointment, but whatever the reason, thinking negatively becomes a pattern that becomes a habit.

You can change that pattern by finding the positive side rather than the negative. The way to change a habit is to replace the old behavior with the new one and practice doing that every time.

Don't Worry, Be Happy

Happiness is one of the keys to life. It has been related to living longer, having more satisfying relationships, and being more resilient. Also, it is a choice to be happy or not. There are two ways to make yourself happy. One is to pursue activities that bring joy into your life. The other is to stop doing whatever you are doing that makes you unhappy. This exercise helps you learn some of the skills to be happier.

The elements of happiness our gratefulness and appreciation for what you have rather than what you don't have. Also, a positive outlook boosts your level of happiness. Optimists are more resilient and more successful. If you do not usually look at the bright side, you may have a habit that needs to be changed.

Changing a habit is accomplished by learning a new pattern to replace the habitual one you use. Then you have to practice the new pattern over and over. Relatively quickly, the new pattern will form a new habit that becomes primary.

Chapter 8:
Change Your Stress Environment

Don't stress about all that you have to do; just enjoy every little step along the way. ~ Matthew Barnett

We have talked about all the consequences of stress. Now let's focus more on some more things you can put into action to reduce stress.

Soul Healing Meditations

An excellent way to lessen stress is meditation. It is a system in which you focus your attention inward to a state of relaxation. Meditation is a practice we've used for thousands of years, and its benefits meet our current needs for relieving anxiety, pain, and depression. It also helps to break the stream of thoughts that flow in and out of our minds.

Research shows the beneficial brain changes continue long after meditating. You will find your attention span and social skills will increase. Plus, it will decrease anxiety, lower aggressive behavior, and antisocial behaviors.

The beauty and simplicity of mediation are that you don't need any special equipment. All that is required is a quiet space and a few minutes each day. Start with five to ten minutes or even try it twice a day. This practice could reduce the costs of medication due to stress. Meditation comes in many forms: here are some of the most common:

Concentration Mediation. This technique involves focusing on a single point. Try to focus on your breathing and repeat a single word. Another option is listening to a repetitive sound. Focusing on the mind is challenging. So, if you find your mind wandering, bring back that thought and refocus on your object of attention. Through this process, your ability to concentrate will improve.

Mindfulness Meditation. Practicing "mindfulness" is staying in the moment. Rather than letting your mind wander, let the thoughts drift through your head. Do not get caught up in the emotional aspect. You can add mindfulness to every moment of your day. Practice it while you are eating, working, or doing household chores like washing dishes. The trick is to stay in the present. Enjoy the current sensations you are experiencing at the moment. Try not to think about past events or imagine future events.

Mindfulness is also an alternative to medication. It is an excellent option for people with anxiety who don't want to take medications for their symptoms. Try a stress reduction class or a stress-management course. It will save you medical care and expenses.

Mindfulness is very beneficial and something that everyone can use. It is a great way to develop an inner balance and relieve anxiety. By reducing your stress response, mindfulness can help regulate the physical stress response. Thus, reducing the risk and severity of stress-related diseases.

Yoga. Although yoga and meditation are two different practices, they do support each other. The posture and concentration required during yoga encourage you to focus and balance. This physical component emphasizes breathing.

Tai Chi. Unlike yoga, Tai Chi alone is not meditative. Instead, it is to focus on the physical and spiritual aspects of life. There are two methods, Neigong and Qigong, which concentrate on "life energy." Both emphasize the importance of body posture, breathing, and meditation to restore energy or "chi."

Guided Imagery. Guided imagery meditation is ideal for beginners. It is more like an exercise for your mind. Often you can do this with a group class or using a phone app or website. The instructor directs you through mind visualizations of sights, sounds, smells, textures. If your mind wanders from the guided instructions, just return your focus and concentration.

Transcendental Meditation. A well-known technique in which you repeat a mantra, a word, or phrase. Learn to quiet your thoughts and achieve greater awareness.

Walking Meditation. Walking meditation turns your focus to both your body and mind as you breathe in time with your footsteps.

Whatever technique you choose, I am confident you will feel a release of tension and anxiety. It does wonders for your body, mind, and spirit. Within a week or two of regular mediation, you should notice a change in your mood and stress level. You should also feel some inner peace and inner poise, even during a busy life.

Be Happy and Joyful

What Comes First – Happiness or Joy? One way to think of happiness is whatever makes us excited about our day. If you cultivate a lifestyle of happiness and joy and apply some of the principles in this book, you will be on our way to living a healthy, stress-less life.

We can create a habit of happiness instead of a pattern of worry. Develop the practice of laughter instead of a tradition of complaining. Most people accept that true happiness is more than positive feelings. It is a sense of "peace" or "contentedness."

Happiness is emotional—and tied to truth. Each of us has feelings with a natural set point—something where our personality comes into focus. Yes, actual events give us a boost, but before long, we swing back toward our natural set point. True happiness lasts longer than a burst of dopamine. Yet it's essential to think of it as something more than only emotion. Happiness is a state of mind. It is a response to our circumstances. It is from what is outside of us.

Joy is a state of being. It encompasses our beliefs, reflections, and a sense of humor. It is how we express our expectations, ideals, and acceptance of what we can't change. Joy is from our internal perspective.

We will experience less stress as we allow this perspective of life to transform us. Our bodies will become less tense, as well. Being at peace has many benefits.

How many people do you know who are happy every day? Cheerful, smiling, and optimistic, who make other people feel the energy. It is a quality gift that we have to cultivate to achieve.

For that matter, are YOU happy? Do you experience joy? Is it possible to cultivate a carefree lifestyle? If you could, how would it affect your stress level?

While it is not possible to have a perfect life, we all face many adverse circumstances. We all have disappointments, but we have a choice on how we choose to respond to them.

How to Develop a Merry Heart Laughter

A happy person knows how to laugh. Studies support the belief that people with a positive perspective tend to be healthier and live longer.

After being diagnosed with a life-threatening autoimmune disease Norman Cousins, became known as a leader of "happiness." His success prompted him to develop his very own laughter therapy. It was a key component of his recovery. His book "Anatomy of an Illness" describes how he used it for better health and it was made it into a movie in 1984.

Our emotional state influences our health. Osteoimmunology has shown that our bone marrow, thymus, and immune cells have receptors. These neurotransmitters imply a "crosstalk" with our immune system organs. This discovery reveals that our gut has an overall impact on health. Our gut and brain are from the same tissue. So, why wouldn't your emotions and mental state affect your health? There have been many studies on the genetic effects of various mental states. Interestingly, different emotional states tend to alter gene expression in different ways.

Practice Forgiveness

Do you keep track of who has wronged you or hurt your feelings? The first step in overcoming deadly emotions is forgiveness instead of anger, resentment, or bitterness. Forgiving is an act of choice. So free your heart of that bondage and let fresh energy flow inside of you.

Take control of your tongue

The words we speak have enormous consequences. "Death and life are in the power of the tongue." A transformed heart will guarantee that the things we speak of are uplifting. Also, what we say can impact our future. "Kind words are like honey."

Surround yourself with positive friends

Words, thoughts, and attitudes are contagious. What can we expect if we surround ourselves with people who are full of negative stories, spread rumors, or use inappropriate language? Happy people tend to have more empathy and are kinder to others.

Spend time with loved ones

Spending time with those we love is an essential element of happiness. Loved ones help to boost our self-esteem and add quality to our life. When we show others that we care, we experience a deep value. It's crucial when we spend the time focusing on them rather than on work or errands. Listen to what they say and respond to their comments.

Connect with Nature

It's not surprising that our ancestors didn't have as much anxiety, stress, or depression as we have today. They spent a lot of time in nature. If we spend most of our time in an office, then drive in our air-conditioned car home to our air-conditioned house. Then we sit in front of our television or play computer games. It's time to consider a change. We are missing out on the pleasure that the great outdoors can bring into our life.

Be in the moment and enjoy the sunshine and fresh air. Observe the trees, whether they are green, shedding, or hibernation. Our connection with nature will be different from our relationship with other things in our life. Nature will always leave you in awe and a peaceful state, while other experiences may make us unhappy.

Take Time to be Grateful

Take time to express our gratefulness for what we have in life. We should not overlook this whether we do it out loud or think it. Practice grateful thoughts during a walk or mediation. Also, keeping a gratitude journal is another way to express being grateful. If we think there is nothing in our life to be grateful for, that's all the more reason to seek gratitude in our life. We may have a lousy job but good health. We may be in a bad relationship but a fulfilling career. Although we need to work on parts of our lives, there are always areas in which we can be grateful.

Feed Your Mind with Positive Thoughts

It's essential to track what we listen to and watch. What enters our minds comes out in actions and affects our wellbeing. Re-evaluate television viewing and commit to turning off anything harmful or negative. Stop listening to depressing music.

If we feed on negative thoughts throughout the day, every trial that comes our way will result in a negative attitude. Rewire your negative thoughts into positive thoughts. It will bring health and healing to the body and the mind.

Our everyday habits and choices influence our wellbeing. Happy people engage in a wide range of practices that seem, well, downright contagious. I hope that as you follow these simple steps, you will discover freshness, joy, renewed zeal, and the healing power of a joyful heart.

Belly Breathing

Breathing is a mechanical act, but most of us don't know how to do it in a way that shift us out of the fight-or-flight condition. Once we learn some deep breathing techniques, it can ease our stress in most situations. We can do it anytime and anywhere. It's a great practice to do while waiting in the car or in a long line at the checkout. I use it when falling asleep at night. It can help quiet our mind and body enough to lead us into a calm sleep.

By taking deep breaths, it shifts our body into a state of relaxation. Deep breathing fills the lungs and stimulates the vagus nerve. This nerve runs from the brain through the neck, lungs, diaphragm, and stomach. It causes our heart and breathing rate to decrease. It also reduces our need for oxygen. Our muscles relax, which in turn releases the tension that we have in our stomach. Our thoughts slow down, and we feel calmer.

I will guide you through several methods of breathing. You can practice on your own by reading through the following exercise. It is refreshing, so give it a try.

Once in a comfortable position, focus on a slow, deep inhale through your nose. If you prefer, you can inhale through your mouth.

Let your belly fill with air. It should rise and expand like an inflated ball as you inhale. Make sure the air goes down deep into your abdomen and fills to your upper chest.

Put one hand on your abdomen and one on your chest. Put your hand on your body so you can gauge whether you're breathing proper. The hand on your chest should remain stationary. The hand on your abdomen should rise and fall with each breath.

Exhale through your mouth. **As you exhale, you should feel your abdomen begin to fall.**

Try to use your diaphragm muscles to force air out of your body.

If you are more comfortable breathing through your nose, you can do that. Exhaling through the mouth is recommended. Make sure that you exhale slow

Remain focused on your breath at every stage of the meditation

Maintain a regular breathing schedule

The best way to get more comfortable with this or any other new habit is by making it a part of your routine and practicing it every day. It will reduce stress and makes you more centered in your day-to-day life.

Try to loosen your abdominal muscles. The goal of soft belly meditation is to have a tool for relieving tension and be focused on your abdomen. When you stress, your muscles get tense. Shallow chest breathing does very little to help relieve that tension.

Focus on the way your abdominal muscles feel before, during, and after each breath. Try to soften your belly with each breath. Let go of tension with the rhythm of breathing in and out.

If you have trouble releasing the tension, try to tighten and release your muscles while you breathe (progressive muscle relaxation).

Choose a mantra to center your thoughts. Repeat a word or phrase that allows you to remain focused on the meditation and bring your mind back from wandering thoughts.

When you have finished, take a moment to sit and observe your breathing. Notice any difference in how you feel? You may want to keep a journal and write down your observations. As you continue to practice, I am sure you will notice improvements in your stress level.

Chapter 9: *Inner Happiness*

Happiness is the ultimate aim of living. Even when making decisions, the best way to decide is by considering the option that will bring you the greatest joy. When you succeed in finding inner happiness, you will have succeeded in overcoming stress in a definitive manner. After all, what is stress other than the absence of happiness? In this chapter, we will look at a few strategies through which you can find inner happiness in life.

Finding Inner Peace

The first source of happiness lies in finding true peace. Being at peace means you remain in a state of spiritual and mental calm even when going through stressful things in your life. Some people keep looking for things to stress them even when everything is going fine. A life spent on the wrong end of the happiness spectrum has convinced them that they can never be happy, so they sabotage their own happiness. If you have ever found yourself in this trap, use the strategies below to work it out and return to true joy.

Zoom Out

Sometimes we get so engrossed in our problems that we fail to see the bigger picture. We only end up making mountains out of molehills because, when a problem is affecting our life at some level, our mind tends to exaggerate the significance and size of the inherent threat. Take a few deep breaths and ask yourself whether the thing over which you are losing sleep will matter in three years. Only things that have a long-term bearing on your future should take your time. Sometimes, the simple act of relaxing and taking a deep breath can go a long way toward calming frayed nerves.

Keep it Simple, Stupid!

This may be a clichéd idea, but it works very effectively. Whether it is your desk at work, your wardrobe at home, or your relationship with your significant other, simplicity has the huge advantage of freeing up the mind. This clarity means that you are in a better position to pinpoint the source of problems in your life and do what you need to do to solve them. Moreover, a decluttered life, whether physical or emotional, is more relaxing.

Cultivate Acceptance

Being hung up over the things that happened in the past is the greatest enemy of true inner peace. This is what causes stress and depression and sucks the joy of living out of life. What most people do not realize is that when you keep stressing about the past, you only extend its chokehold over your life.

A better strategy is to simply let go. And even though it might take you some time to get to the point of true and utter acceptance, it is a journey you should really pursue. As soon as you start going the acceptance way rather than questioning God and the universe, you take back the power that was once yours.

At the end of the day, regardless of your belief system, the only things you can control are your own actions and reactions. Accepting this fact will help you avoid wasting your life trying to answer questions you cannot or solve problems beyond your abilities.

Ask, Do Not Presume

This is a huge problem in relationships. You see or hear something, interpret it one way, then proceed to overthink it and act out for a few hours or a few days. In the end, you realize that your own prejudices made you blow purely innocent words or actions out of proportion. It is so much better to seek clarification.

Find an Escape

What do you do when you are feeling overwhelmed? Having an escape gives you a sure way of buying yourself time before confronting that huge problem stressing you out. Simply curling up with a good novel or watching a good movie might make a huge difference—you really should try it.

Living a Purposeful Life

You cannot be truly happy if you are not living the life you are meant to live. In other words, either you are living a purposeful life, or you are not living at all. In this section, we will look at some of the ways through which you can activate the purpose of your life and live accordingly.

Spiritual Enlightenment

One of the greatest advantages of meditation is that it helps you to tap into your superconscious mind. This allows you to get in touch with your true self and discover your life's purpose. But discovering your purpose in life is not enough; you must dedicate your life to fulfilling your purpose if you are to attain true happiness. When you are doing what you are meant to do, every moment becomes a form of enjoyment rather than work. This makes it easier for you to get into the state of flow, which increases your productivity, boosts your income, and further adds to your sense of happiness and fulfillment.

Building Your Decision-Making Abilities

Decision-making affects the overall quality of your life in two ways. The first and foremost way is through the process of making a decision itself. If your decision-making skills are not at an acceptable level, you will struggle with every decision, stressing yourself out and bringing your level of inner happiness down.

The second way through which decision-making affects inner happiness is in how it attracts karma into our lives. You see, even though you have complete free will, the universe still keeps a balance sheet of your actions. At some point in the future, the scales will be balanced, and you will receive goodness for every good deed you have done and pay the cost of the bad. So, instead of blaming others for the things you have done out of your own free will, start doing things deserving of good karma. This is the only way to set the scales right.

Unlocking Your Life's Potential

Nothing in life is sadder than missed opportunities. When you hesitate and lose that huge deal that you have made your career, you will regret it for the rest of your life. Applied to life, the inability to attain your highest potential haunts your mind, body, and spirit. For as long as you remain conscious of your true purpose in life and are not pursuing it, you will never quite know inner peace and happiness. The neglected dreams and goals of your life will haunt you every step of the way.

Embrace Your True Self

True happiness comes only from being true to yourself. Many people waste their lives by living it by someone else's standards. This only creates regrets and unhappiness later on in life. In this section, we will identify a few strategies for embracing your true self and living that way full-time.

Be True to Your Inner Being

Understanding who you are is the first step to self-realization. In a world where everyone is trying to define you and put you in a box, tapping deep within to find your identity is indispensable. You can do this by listening to the inner voice and blocking out any other voices that might be trying to control the way you live your life.

Your inner voice will help you to determine your deepest desires, likes, dislikes, and wants. Even better, it cannot judge you because it is essentially you. The only thing for you to do after discovering who you are is to become unapologetically true to yourself. We go into so much trouble trying to make ourselves something we are not in the hope that other people will like us - while we just need to be true to ourselves.

Avoid Comparisons

In a world where we are more socially connected than ever before, it can be very hard to remain authentic when others in our circles are living the flashy or "cooler" lifestyle. In fact, comparing is what makes embracing your true self (and thus finding inner happiness) so difficult. It is human nature to be competitive and want to be the best at everything, so when we see someone else who is better at something we care about, the first instinct is usually jealousy. This makes way for comparisons, which are essentially the mind's way of reminding us that we are worse than everyone else.

I am not saying that you cannot observe (or even comment on) other people's abilities and strengths. Comparisons only become poisonous when accompanied by jealousy, when they take you off the path of pursuing your own dreams, or when they are done too frequently. The worst thing about comparing is that it blinds you to your own strengths by making you dwell on other people.

Commit to Your Decisions

Committing to the choices you make is what reinforces your true nature. People who are not true to their identity will always have trouble following through on their decisions because those decisions do not reflect their true wishes. Start by committing to the smallest choices, such as a restaurant to eat at and then move up until you are taking out a mortgage. The more you follow through on decisions, make mistakes, and work to correct them, the closer you will get to your authentic self and the better your decisions will reflect it.

Embrace Change

At some point in life, you will change so much that you will become almost the exact opposite of the person you were before. Your physical features may change, as will your principles, values, and beliefs. Sometimes this can be very scary, especially if you care about being true to your real self. However, when you recognize that change is inevitable, you will more readily embrace the changes that occur in your life. As long as your progress is toward the light, there is nothing wrong with making a few alterations to your character here and there. Just make sure that you own the change rather than surrendering to it.

Practice Gratitude

For people who have been unhappy for too long, unhappiness becomes a part of their identity. They find themselves being unhappy even when things are going really well simply because they do not know how to appreciate things. This is where gratitude comes in. The whole idea of counting your blessings actually works. So, if you want to attain true inner happiness, stop obsessing over all the things that have gone wrong or could go wrong in the future and appreciate the stuff that worked out.

The exact gratitude exercises you can perform to increase your level of appreciation and happiness in your life include:

The Five-Item Checklist

Every night before going to bed, sit down and list five things about the day for which you are grateful. They can range from good health and food to a promotion and healthy relationships. Writing down this list reminds you that there are things that are okay in your life even when you are going through a trying moment. With time, you will start to witness more hope, peace, and happiness bubbling from deep within your heart.

Appreciate the People Who Make Your Life Easier

Whether it is the waiter who serves your coffee in the morning or the person who delivers a long-anticipated parcel, make sure you let people know that you value their help. Sometimes a simple thank-you will suffice, but sometimes you might need to do something a lot more thought-out for people who went out of their way to make your life easier.

The universe might forgive you for forgetting to give thanks for good health and a good life, but people will never forget (or forgive) ingratitude. After all, there is nothing like selfless altruism—everyone expects some sort of reward for helping out. The best way to reward help is by expressing your gratitude in an overt and clear way. The bigger the good deed, the greater the reward should be. Because, believe me, the person on the other side will be expecting that reward. Even if you cannot give value for value, the amount of thought you put into your gratitude will say a lot.

Meditate

The techniques above will help you get into an attitude of gratitude, but if you want to change your life and appreciate its richness, you should aim for a complete mental shift. Become a glass half-full kind of person by practicing the gratitude meditation exercises outlined below. Gratitude meditation seeks to make you more consciously aware of all the things that are going right with your life.

Follow the steps of mindfulness meditation for posture, relaxation, and deep breaths.

- When you start meditating, think about all the things for which you are grateful rather than emptying your mind of all thoughts.
- Let these thoughts of gratitude fill your mind, including the sensations of receiving the good deeds behind the gratitude.
- Follow through with about five minutes of experiencing the sensations of gratitude alone without the things for which you are grateful. This embeds gratitude deep within your consciousness and helps you to remain in that state a lot longer.
- Practice this form of meditation as often as possible.

Chapter 10:
Tips for Building Self-Social Confidence

Being social and interacting with other people in social gatherings can be fun and exciting! However, this environment can be scary and cause anxiety for some people. Nevertheless, you can overcome these feelings of exhaustion and anxiety in social interaction if you build your social confidence. The following are some of the tips that can help you to build your social confidence.

Improve yourself to build your overall confidence

Strive to achieve more to become a better version of yourself. You can start by doing those things that make you feel proud of yourself. Go for further studies and earn that degree you dream of, exercise and eat healthily to become physically fit so you have that dream body, change your hairstyle and look new, take up dance lessons and be a great dancer, get a job and start earning money or start a business.

Do those things that will make you be socially accepted; this means that you have to provide value for society to accept you. Value can be anything that others will find worthy. Having a great body is very attractive and is value. Likewise to being a good dancer, people will enjoy watching you or dancing with them, and this is also value.

The bottom-line is to improve yourself so you can have value that society accepts and will boost your social confidence. It is doable, it's just a matter of mindset and attitude!

Socialize more

To develop any skill, you need to practice it. Look out for social events in your area and attend them alone. Walking with friends when going to events will never give you the chance of socializing by yourself. It will hinder your progress towards gaining social confidence.

When interacting with other people try to keep a confident posture and body language and maintain good eye contact during a conversation. Speak clearly and not too fast; and if you feel tense, try to take slow deep breaths. When interacting with people and making new friends, do not have any expectations from them; your aim should only be to feel good about yourself.

Do not limit yourself to talking to those people who can offer you something only - talk to everyone from that grocery woman to the elderly neighbors and even your employees or workmates. Worry less about the outcome of the interaction but rather enjoy the moment of socializing and have fun!

After getting the courage to talk to everyone and interacting with new people confidently, you can plan a social event in your place where you can sit and enjoy some laughter. Invite your new friends and get to know more about them and even do things that you enjoy together, like playing a sport. This move can give you a leadership role in a social set up, and people will look forward to the meetings you plan.

Design and deliver a presentation on your topic of expertise

What is your area of expertise? Do people come to you for some knowledge about something? If the answer is yes, use this opportunity to sharpen your social confidence and social leadership. You can compile some information on the topic of your expertise and deliver it to your audience. This will boost your social confidence as well as communication skills, and you will have a sense of authority.

After delivering the presentation, what is the reaction of your audience? Making a presentation in front of an audience will give the audience an intuition of who you are as a person and will make them approach you more comfortably. This will enable you to show your uniqueness. You will achieve confidence in your area of expertise and in a comfortable environment.

Manage your emotions

The social set up comes with different kinds of verbal and non-verbal language like facial expressions and voice tone that you will have to analyze before you respond. Being in social places requires a great sense of emotional control. People do not like to associate with someone who gets furious easily and throws tantrums. Whenever conflicts arise in your presence, try to remain calm and argue constructively.

You cannot control other people's opinions. Sometimes people will tease you to joke with you, so do not be too hard on yourself and others. They may laugh but that does not necessarily mean they intended to hurt you. So laugh it off and do not let anyone intimidate you with his or her toxic behavior.

Go to networking events

Networking events can be useful in building social confidence. Find one that suits your needs and try socializing with new people. The more you interact freely, the more you are building your social confidence that can also lead to social leadership. Eventually, you will find it easy to express yourself.

Do the right thing

Your actions define your character! Always aspire to do the right thing even when it is not in your best interest or even if it is hard. Later, you will be happy and proud of yourself because of the sound decisions you made concerning your actions.

Learn to handle failure

We sometimes face rejection at some point in our lives but this does not mean you are unlikable or are unable to make friends. This feeling can cripple you, and you may even feel like you cannot do it. Do not despair; instead, take a moment, look deep inside yourself, collect yourself once again, and keep going. Even the most successful people have failed once, but they kept working on improving themselves and taking risks because their goals were greater than their fear of failure. Visualize your dreams, put your fears aside, and keep pushing forward.

Socially confident individuals turn negative responses into opportunities for learning and doing better. They make comments like, "well, I'll do better next time."

Do not listen to naysayers

Some people will try to discourage you from reaching your goals by telling you that it is not possible, so and so tried and they failed, or it has never been done before. They will tell you that you are over-ambitious or your goal is too big and unachievable. Do not give the negative voices room in your mind. Just tell them that it is doable and that you believe in your goal.

Remember, no human is limited. Your goals depend on your will and determination to achieve them. What other people think about you does not matter, but what you think about yourself does. If you think you can do it, then you can do it. Just believe in yourself and keep going.

Act confident

When nothing else seems to be working, you can fake self-social confidence. You can fake it until you make it! Hold your head high and get a confident posture and body language. Maintain good eye contact and a smile when taking part in a conversation. A smile will lighten your mood and make other people see a self-confident person. A happy face is more approachable! The more you act having self-confidence, the more your actual self-confidence rises.

Stay with uplifting people

The attitudes of our inner circle play a role in defining our self-confidence. What they say about our performance affects our self-social confidence either positively or negatively. When they make good comments, it increases our self-confidence, and when the comments are bad, they lower our self-social confidence. Negative feedback gives us a negative perception of ourselves.

Too many positive comments on our performance can also lead to being overconfident and this can lead to unrealistic self-perception and vice versa. Although positive feedback motivates you, it should be real.

Get organized

Disorganization and chaos can lead to self-doubt. When you are organized, it gives you a sense of self-perception that says you are in control of your life. This positive perception of yourself will boost your self-confidence. Confidence thrives in an organized environment!

Focus on your success and not the failure

Focusing on your failures will kill your sense of self-confidence. Fill your mind with your great achievements and success. List your successful achievements and look at them daily. This will build your self-social confidence. Change your mental perception to build a positive attitude.

Strategies For Improving Your Social Confidence

Some people prefer being alone rather than being in the company of a group. Such people will sit in a corner at a party and enjoy their drink alone, staying away from the crowd. They simply like watching others do but do not want to be part of the interaction. You can only be socially confident if you have a confident outlook and practice improving your social skills. The following are some tips that can help you be socially confident.

Put on a confident outlook: first, you need to *accept who you are*. If you are an introvert and enjoy being alone and doing your own thing, do not force yourself to be outgoing. This will make the situation worse, and it will stress you! However, you can introduce yourself gradually to social life by attending the social events you enjoy. Since you understand your introvert nature, try to have meaningful conversations at those social events that you attend.

Know the benefits of confidence: interacting with people in a way that interests them will boost your social confidence. This could be through the assets you have like an attractive body or making them laugh when having conversations. This is social competence, and it is essential in boosting self-social confidence in social gatherings. Having social competence will make you more likable and approachable.

Get rid of negative thoughts: if you do not have a self-perception of social confidence, you will be looking for proof to confirm your belief. How you think about yourself determines your self-confidence. Negative thoughts increase self-doubt and kill self-confidence. If you find yourself having a negative thought about yourself, stop that thought and ask yourself what evidence is there to support the thought.

Test your conviction: examine the evidence you found to support your negative thoughts and see if it is an outcome of those things we can't control. Understand that how other people react is not up to you; it's up to them. Be kind and compassionate to them and try to find out the cause of their reaction. For example, if someone laughed while you are talking and you thought they were laughing at you, ask yourself if the laughter could be associated with other things. Maybe the person saw something funny and he/she couldn't control the laughter.

Be kind and compassionate to others: being compassionate when interacting with others is a very good social skill that can build social confidence. If you intend to interact meaningfully with others, then you should practice empathy. For example, if your colleague has not come to work, call or text him/her to ask if he/she is okay. This will send be good gesture, indicating that you are compassionate and caring.

Check your intentions: sometimes, people do not get along well no matter how much they try to be social. This is very natural, and it happens to all of us at some point in our social interactions. To build social confidence, you need to understand that you are not responsible for other people's emotions and actions. For example, if you greet someone and he/she does not respond, brush it off and keep going. You will find someone with whom you can get along and be friends.

Show interest in other people: other people should feel comfortable and valued when around you. Social competence is the ability to make others feel comfortable, valued and heard. Get to know the right verbal and non-verbal language to use when you are in social places. When engaging in a conversation, maintain good eye contact and do not cross your arms as it often makes some people uncomfortable.

Emphasize non-verbal communication through body language: you should stand or sit in a posture that signifies self-confidence. Good body posture will boost your confidence and make you look comfortable. For example, a good handshake can make you connect with other people and its memory will last. Maintain good eye contact but do not stare for long because it makes some people uncomfortable. You can alternate with staring at the shoulder or forehead. Smile to show that you are enjoying the moment. Remember a happy face signifies confidence. Maintain a still posture without swaying the body or looking nervous. If you feel tense, take slow deep breaths to calm you down.

Speak clearly: how you speak can determine your social confidence. If you want to look confident, you need to speak audibly and clearly for everyone to hear you. Your voice should not be too high or low but you can practice tone variation to portray confidence and assertiveness. Mumbling is not good, and it can send a message that you are not interested in the conversation.

Your speaking pace should be reasonable: it should be slow enough for others to grasp what you are communicating. Remember that it should not be too slow because the conversation will be boring and people will lose interest. If you speak too fast, people will miss some key points in your conversation and this might make them lose interest in the conversation. A fast pace signifies nervousness and anxiety. For a normal speaking pace, take slow deep breaths during the entire conversation. If you realize that your pace has suddenly increased, pause and breathe before moving on.

Be a good listener: when someone is speaking, give him/her your full attention and visualize what he/she is trying to communicate. This can make you empathetic, and it will help you give appropriate responses. Listening actively to others while they talk shows that you respect and care about their opinions, and this will increase your social confidence. If you are tense or nervous, you will likely concentrate on your tension and not the speaker; this can make others feel like you do not value them. Never interrupt the speaker; say what you want when the speaker finishes talking.

Practice confidence and go to social events: the best way to develop a skill is through practice. You should attend several gatherings of your liking and interact with people until you develop your social skills and improve your social confidence. Over time, you will feel more comfortable and your anxiety levels will drop. Start a meaningful conversation with greetings and comment about the event. You can then introduce yourself once you get the attention of the other person.

Role-play: you can practice social skills when you are with a friend or family member. He/she will pretend to be someone from a social event, and you will start the conversation by introducing yourself. You should practice speaking confidently with a good posture that portrays confidence and comfort. You should end your conversation by saying "it was a pleasure meeting you hope we shall meet again."

Let a friend help you socialize: your friend can take you to social events to meet his/her friends. This will help in improving your social confidence because the introduction will be easy and they will not look like strangers to you. Your friend will do the introduction then you can join the conversation at the appropriate time.

Socialize in new places: once you have gained some confidence, you can go to social events alone without a friend. For example, you can join sporting clubs of your interest and work on meeting new people and interacting with them. You will eventually find people who click well with you, and you will have achieved your goal of gaining social confidence. This move may lead you towards getting social leadership.

Conclusion

We all deal with self-doubt. It's not something that's actually going to go away, so you've got to figure out how you will reframe it. How are you going to use self-doubt as a tool to motivate you, make you stay driven, and make sure that even in those things you're scared of, you approach them with courage? Self-doubt isn't something you should be upset about. I go onto arenas where there are 25,000 people in the audience, and while I am backstage, I have anxiety and concern. Am I going to do a good job today?

Everybody has self-doubt. The challenge is that some people think they don't need to have it, and some are using it as a tool to stop moving towards their dreams instead of progressing toward their goals. So here are four big ideas on how to better deal with self-doubt so you can still go after your dreams.

#1: Reframe confidence

You have to reframe confidence. A lot of people say, "I'm just not confident. I wish I were more confident, and I wish I had more fire. I wish I believed in myself more. I always worry about myself. I never believe in myself. I'm always selling myself short, and I never give myself credit. I just quit."

I think what happens is they just never really learned what absolute confidence is. We did the most extensive study ever been done on high performers worldwide, and what we learned is that the most successful people in the world approach confidence in the same way. They believe in their ability to figure things out. It doesn't mean they don't have self-doubt, but they think, "I can figure things out. Give me enough time, energy, resources, mentorship, support, and I can figure anything out." You have to start believing that.

As much as you spend time questioning yourself, you have to think, "Can I remember the things in the past I figured out that I wasn't prepared for?" You've done projects in the past and you've been in situations where you had no idea how to handle it, but you figured it out. Take confidence in that. The next time you go into a situation, and all you can do freak out, I want you to remember all those times when you did overcome the doubts and the anxiety, the lack of skills, the unknowns, and you still pulled it off.

There are more times in your life that you overcame self-doubt than you give yourself credit for. Maybe you showed up that one time to school, and you were self-doubting, but people liked you, and you were just fine. Perhaps one time you went into a project, and you knew you didn't know how to do it, but by the end of that week, you figured it out. You have to have a memory for the things you did overcome, as much as you worry about the things you lack. If your thought pattern is constantly repeating, "I lack, I lack, I lack, I lack, I lack..." Of course you're going to self-doubt all the time, to a degree where you stop trying. If you can have that positive self-talk and remind yourself of all the times you overcame what you did not know, it will lead to genuine self-confidence.

You might find yourself saying, "You know what? I believe in my ability to figure things out. Even if I have some doubts about how it might go or doubts about how things might turn out, I know I will figure it out. Give me enough time, energy, effort, resources, and support, and I can do it." That's genuine self-confidence. Even though you have doubts, the next time you're going into a situation where you have doubt, I want you to say, "You know what? I'll figure it out," and trust in that.

#2: Show up with intention

If you want to deal with self-doubt, you absolutely must start entering each day with more intention. One of the reasons we don't believe in ourselves is because we're just all over the place.

Sometimes you're relaxed in one situation, but you're dumb in another. Sometimes you don't do well here, but you do well there. What happens is that so many people are going through the motions, or they're just showing up in life every single day. They're reacting and because they're constantly reacting, they don't have character.

They haven't determined: who am I? Who am I going to act like in this situation? Who am I going to behave like in this situation? How am I going to treat people in this situation? Because they haven't shown up with intention and sought to live out that intention, they feel a lot of discord in life. They don't know who they are because they just keep showing up and reacting to what's there. But guess what? What's there is always different.

The world is constantly changing, people are always changing, and situations are continually changing. If all you're doing is showing up and reacting, thinking, "I guess I'll just go through it and see how it goes," you';; never form an intentional character.

Of course, you doubt yourself because every situation is different, and you can never have complete certainty. But you can have strength inside. From now on, wake up every day, and say, "I'm going to be these three words today." Just set the words, "I'm going to be fun, I'm going to be playful, I'm going to be kind." And that day, you are fun, playful, and kind. And the next day, you say, "I'm going to be patient, thoughtful, and appreciative," and you act patient, thoughtful, and appreciative. You do this over and over and over again, setting an intention for who you want to be. Set an intention and be that.

Do that in more situations in your life and more days, weeks, months, and years, and you'll be more confident in yourself because you know that you can direct your mind, emotions, and body to be the person you want to be. The more often you do that, the more authentic, genuine self-confidence will come into your life.

#3: Get clarity, get a plan, get momentum

You need to get clarity, you need to get a plan, and you need to gain momentum. Many people have self-doubt in their lives because they don't have clarity. Many people wander into a situation and have a lot of self-doubts because they didn't sit down and plan it out. They didn't prepare. They didn't ask mentors or emulate others or do the research to figure out, "I should do a, b, c, d, and e." If you don't know the steps to success, of course, you'll have more self-doubt. If you don't have the plan, if you don't have the map; if you don't know what you're doing, of course, you're going to have more self-doubt.

Decide to build a plan, even if you have to ask for help. Ask, "Hey, guys, how would you do this? What would be your first step? What would be your second step?" I'm always asking that. Even at this stage in my career, I'm still saying, "Hey guys, if you were going to launch this, how would you do it? If you were going to promote that, how would you do it? If you were going to create this thing, how would you do it? If you were going to build this team or build that business, what would you do?" I always try to get the map before I enter the woods so I have the steps. Know the path because if you can remove the doubt about the course, you'll have more confidence in yourself.

#4: Learn vs. judge

The fourth big idea (this one is so straightforward, but I think people don't do it) i you need to learn versus judge when it comes to your behaviors and results in life. Start a Sunday review. Sit down and evaluate how you did this last week. How did you do Monday, Tuesday, Wednesday, Thursday, and Friday?

What situations did you do well in? What conditions could you have done better in? What did you learn about yourself? And use that review session not to beat yourself up, or be mad at yourself, or to stir self-talk filled with self-hatred, but rather to say, "What did I learn about who I am, and what I prefer in life? What did I learn about what I like? What did I learn about the best of me, and what did I learn about the go-through-the-motions me? Where did I feel down? Where did I feel confident?"

Start experimenting with how you view yourself by doing a better job of reviewing your week. People don't have as confident a mentality as they should because they're just barreling through, oblivious to how much they've grown. Instead of judging yourself, have an entire self-evaluation session every week: How did I do, what did I learn? In that personal development, look at yourself objectively, without judging or giving negative labels. Observe how you're going through your life, and then tell yourself, "Next time, I'll do this differently, and next time, I'll do this, and next time, I'll do that." That's a learning mentality versus a judgment mentality.

A judgment mentality is: I was an idiot. I was stupid. I didn't like myself. I look stupid. People are going to mock me; they're going to hate me. Such judgmental self-talk leads to low self-confidence. Most people spend most of their time criticizing themselves. Their self-talk is negative instead of learning-oriented. So next time you're plagued with self-doubt, think of a few of these things:

Reframe confidence, don't think you have to be completely confident. Just say, "You know what? I'm going to figure my way through this. It's going to be okay. I'm going to trust. I've figured out things in the past, and I'll figure out this one."

Make sure that you start each day or walk into each situation with a little more intention. Who do you want to be and live like that more consistently because it start to form the character you can take confidence in.

Make sure you get to your plan and take the steps. Then you get a little momentum because it comes with more confidence and a little more self-assuredness.

Do you know when you're going to be the proudest of yourself? When you find real, genuine self-confidence and grow at the rate and the speed you genuinely desire. So keep learning, my friend, and listen: you're stronger than you think, and the future holds good things for you.

Burnout

The 22 Most Effective Methods to Recover From Burnout

Declan Evans

Introduction

Spoiler alert: if you've been feeling irritated, exhausted, and unable to find satisfaction in your work for a few weeks — or months — there's a good chance you're suffering from burnout.

Burnout is one of those words that gets thrown around so much that it has lost some of its meaning, so let's start with the basics. Burnout refers to prolonged stress without enough recovery time between periods of stress. The key to being burnout-free is to have a good work-life balance. Sometimes recovering from burnout involves time away from the workplace — and it might feel like you're being punished when you're forced off the job. In reality, taking time off to recover is good for your company.

Some people never experience burnout because they have the foresight to plan their time and set boundaries; others don't take enough breaks. But no matter what your circumstances are, everyone needs to know what kinds of things make them feel burned out to recognize warning signs early on.

Burnout doesn't happen just because you work hard: many people work hard and never experience burnout. Burnout can only be diagnosed when you feel exhausted yet have no desire to keep working. That's when you know it's time to take a break.

It may seem like we're all living in a 24/7 whirlwind of stress, but it's not just you — burnout is very much a thing. And according to an article from the American Psychological Association, it's more common than you might think.

Types of Burnout

The three types of burnout are physical, emotional, and mental. Physical burnout occurs when "a person experiences high levels of physical tension and fatigue," emotional burnout happens when "a person feels their job has drained their energy and emotions." Mental burnout is characterized by "persistent feelings of ineffectiveness. "

Now, even though burnout is a serious condition, it's not something to be afraid of—it doesn't mean you're worthless. That's what makes this article so interesting. Check out the list below to learn about some ways to fight the burnout epidemic:

1. **Physical burnout -** This is very common, considering that an estimated 86% of employees have reported experiencing their work as an energy drain. It can also be a serious health hazard as well. According to the article, "people who work at high effort jobs over 40 hours per week are more likely to report symptoms of depression. Our bodies were not built to work all day, every day. It's important to take regular breaks to reduce levels of fatigue and prevent burnout.

1. **Emotional burnout -** Many people expect colleagues to be there for support, but it's all too easy to get stressed out by other people's expectations or incompetence. And that can drain your emotional energy. According to the article, "high levels of emotional exhaustion and depression are correlated with emotional burnout among workers. Being emotionally drained can put an employee at risk of divorce as well as other mental and physical health problems." As a result, over 16% of employees claim to be connected to one or more coworkers

emotionally. Nearly 1/3 of employees are so drained from coworkers that they feel personally victimized by them.

2. **Mental burnout -** It's often about what you value. When you have a job you don't value or aren't passionate about, it's very easy to get depressed and angry about the situation you're in—and that's the beginning of burnout. According to the article, "when employees experience low levels of job satisfaction, they are more likely to become depressed and report physical symptoms such as headaches and back pain. These mental health problems are linked to physical sickness or injury among workers." Over 17% of employees report being depressed or frustrated about work, and almost 9% are so stressed out at work that they can't concentrate properly.

Burnout sign and symptoms

If you've been reading about what burnout is and the different types of people at risk, it may not be hard to figure out if you're one of them. The difficult part can be figuring out how to detect—and hopefully reverse—burnout before any permanent damage is done.

Here are five signs that mean you're experiencing burnout:

- **Apathy:** You don't have the will or motivation to do anything anymore. You don't care about work, family, or friends. If someone needs a hand with something and asks for your help, your response is more likely to be "why not?" than "yes."

- **Unhappiness:** You're feeling miserable at your work. You may still be getting things done, but something's not right. Your emotions are down, and you don't think things will get better soon.

- **Fatigue:** It doesn't matter what time of day it is, how much sleep you got, or how much coffee you drink; your energy level is low, and you're running on empty. You can't seem to get up in the morning too early to start your day. You can go all day and be exhausted by nightfall.

- **Overwhelmed:** You feel like there's so much you need to do every day that it makes you feel overwhelmed all the time. You feel like your job has become too much, and there's no way you can get it done.

- **Negativity:** This is also a big sign of burnout. You're just not a happy person to be around anymore. People who know you outside of work or outside of being sick may complain that you're not the same person they know in different circumstances.

- **Feeling Helpless:** You don't have any control over anything anymore, and it's driving you crazy! You feel like there's no way to make things better, and your only option is to wait until something changes or someone else takes action.

- **Depression:** Burnout isn't all about physical exhaustion. Some people's bodies don't feel tired, but they feel very mentally and emotionally down on themselves. They might find things harder to do, and they aren't positive or happy anymore. They get irritated at everything and everyone around them.

Method 1:
Talk to your Family Doctor

If you're feeling the effects of burnout, it's time you talked to your family doctor. Don't worry, it's not an emergency – but it is a serious medical condition that may require some time off work, so don't let it get too far out of hand.

If the symptoms I just mentioned sound familiar, your family doctor can help solve them. Talk to them about a possible change in workload or schedule and see if they can recommend resources for relaxation or stress relief that might be helpful to you. If you're working too hard, it's time to make a change. Your family doctor can help with that.

Research has shown that over 60% of family doctors experience burnout at some point in their careers. You shouldn't be hesitant to ask them about it because they can help put you on the path to a happier, healthier life.

Suicide is often considered a last resort for people who are feeling helpless and hopeless. Don't let burnout get that bad for you. Talk to your family doctor about it today and start moving towards a better life.

He/she runs things like a tight ship

Have you heard the expression "He/she runs things like a tight ship?" When a ship is run by a captain or crew who refuses to take time off and insists on running the ship at a breakneck speed no matter what, the result can be disastrous. There are, in fact, two kinds of burnout — burnout for the captain and crew of an overworked ship and for those who work too hard but are not in charge of anything — like nurses or doctors. But both types have similar symptoms and effects.

Burnout for the captain and crew of an overworked ship starts to develop after very long work weeks with short breaks. The alternative is to slow down, but that might cost the company money or put the company's bottom line at risk. Either way, burnout for captains and crew will likely culminate in serious health problems — heart disease, emergency room visits, missed days of work — or even being written up or even fired. This kind of burnout is more common among captains and crew who feel powerless or just don't know how to speak up about their concerns.

Some of those breakdowns and tragedies might be avoided if captains and crew had a little tenderness for their bodies. The same thing goes for doctors and nurses under constant work deadlines and has to walk a tightrope of being nice to their patients.

Burnout for those who aren't in charge of anything like captains or crew is different. In this case, it's more common among workers who are doing multiple jobs that require different skill sets like a nurse who also has to treat a patient's family member when the family member needs help. There can also be generational differences, so don't assume this kind of burnout will occur only among older workers.

Family Physician

Many young family physicians (FPs) like me have two jobs. I love working in primary care and am lucky to do it year-round. But having a second job as a physician assistant (PA) has its challenges, like arranging my schedules to accommodate the PA schedule and dealing with the extra stress of being recognized as a busy FNP while also being an active FNP who still manages to see patients. As an FNP, I've seen firsthand. A colleague on the floor saw me coming out of the exam room and said, "Hang in there! You're hired!" when she was preparing other residents for their call shifts.

So, things can get pretty busy in a few ways. But to help you, I offer you three questions: How hard is it to get your work done? How well does your workflow? How well do you feel when you leave the office each day?

Okay, I'm going to break this down for you. When I think about my job, I feel like there are three parts: taking care of family, taking care of patients, and taking care of myself. Taking care of family means doing the "homework" when I need to take time off from working with my patients and make sure my family gets enough attention and support. The question for me is, how much time can I take before I get myself into trouble?

The second question is about the flow of my work. If it's like a river, then I'm trying to find a way to keep it flowing as smoothly as possible. Sometimes these currents can be strong and unpredictable. Maybe you need a time-out, or maybe there's something for the current to run into that will divert its energy or put out some rocks before it goes over them.

The third question is about my feeling of well-being after each day's work. If it feels like I'm going through the motions, I need to examine myself to see where the trouble is. Do I feel stuck in a rut? Am I juggling too many balls in the air?

If your answer is "no," then your job is not a tight ship, or you're running it like a tight ship. You might even be at risk for burnout. Talk to your family physician about it, and they can help you figure out how to change your pace so that you can get healthy again and feel better not only for yourself but also for those around you.

What family doctor can do about burnout?

Burnout for nurses or doctors who work too hard can be avoided if the doctor or nurse gets plenty of rest and takes frequent breaks. Taking frequent breaks can be difficult for a doctor or nurse who is overworked and finds the hours long, but if they don't take enough rest breaks, they'll be more likely to get sick and therefore miss work due to illness.

Getting into a rhythm of getting plenty of rest and taking frequent breaks is easier than it sounds if you're not fighting work stresses. If you are fighting work stresses and things aren't going well at your job, you may need to consider looking for other work (or not).

But even for those who do, burnout can set in. If that's you, then you may feel exhausted all the time, you might have trouble getting through a normal day at work, and you're probably doing less work than usual. You may be making mistakes at work because your hands shake and your head is spinning so much it's hard to concentrate, or your family might notice that something is wrong with you, like that you seem irritable all the time. The anxiety and stress of burnout will likely get worse if nothing changes.

So, talk to your family doctor about all of this and see if they can help. It may not be as serious as what I've described, but if you're feeling symptoms like these and you don't know how to stop them, then it's time to talk to your family doctor about burnout. And remember, don't let burnout get too out of hand; take that time off when necessary.

A family doctor can help a whole family have a better life. A family physician knows about nutrition, exercise, balance, and many other aspects of health that can enhance an entire family's well-being. When you go to the doctor, you see that they're busy, and we all know how busy doctors are, so we put up with the fact that they don't have time to answer all our questions. But when you go to the doctor because of something like not feeling well or having a heart issue, they're more likely to listen and help you get better.

Method 2:
See a Psychologist

If you've been contemplating seeing a psychologist but have been hesitant, wondering about burnout, we assure you that it is normal. In fact, by speaking to a psychologist, you can help stay in the healthiest mindset possible and prevent burnout. Don't be afraid to speak up about what's bothering you with an experienced professional who understands that it can be incredibly difficult work. Psychiatrists are there to help, and they want nothing more than for you to feel better about yourself and your mental health.

There are many reasons for psychologists to burn out in their practice. Some may point to the heavy workload that includes listening to hours of non-stop complaints from clients and sitting through many emotional sessions without any breaks in between sessions. However, before you decide against seeing a psychologist and instead resort to hypnotism or quitting altogether, you might want to consider consulting with a fellow professional first.

Reasons to see a psychologist cure burnout

A psychologist will know the signs of burnout and may be able to help you avoid it completely. If your mental health is suffering, it will become difficult to do your working tasks. During a doctor-patient relationship, it is important that the patient feel safe and can share things freely to heal quickly.

One good way of curing burnout for a psychologist is by counseling. After counseling, a person can feel an instant relief by venting out their feelings and getting practical and helpful tips on improving their situation in life.

With counseling sessions, many psychologists can manage their work pressures better with improved time management skills. If you are a psychologist, you should remember that the most important thing to do in your practice is to remain calm and patient.

Occasionally, you may feel exhausted with your work, and it is okay to take some time off. It's important to take rest breaks as frequently as possible to prevent burnout. If you feel burned out, then there's a high chance that it will affect the quality of your work or even endanger it if not taken care of on time. If you suspect that you're feeling burned out mentally, then find time for yourself as soon as possible.

Counseling session for burnout

Counseling is the best method for a psychologist to tackle burnout. The benefits of counseling are so important that it should not be taken lightly. With counseling, you will answer your questions and learn more about yourself and your relationships with others.

Getting counseling once a week is more than enough for burnt-out psychologists. Once you're ready to see a therapist, you should find calm and patient, as these are very important factors in maintaining psychological health.

A therapist will help you feel secure and safe enough to open up to them from the session's start. In a counseling session, the therapist helps you to find out more about yourself and examine everything that is going on in your mind.

You can expect a therapist to answer your questions and provide advice on your situation. Besides simply talking, therapists can also ask you questions regarding simple tasks and draw them out from you may help you.

Get to know yourself and what you're thinking more often. Don't be afraid to let go of the things that are getting on your nerves and those you don't like. Tell your therapist about some of your past saddest moments that have made you feel different in a way that may be difficult for others to understand at first glance.

Examine yourself more thoroughly to determine why you still feel this way despite how many years have passed. Learn how to recognize suicidal thoughts, depression, or other symptoms related to burnout so it doesn't become a problem anymore for you or someone else in your vicinity.

Method 3:
Do Yoga

It's no secret that a lot of people are feeling a little burnt out these days. We're always on the go, trying to keep up with work, family, and friends. But it sometimes feels like we don't have the energy to do anything else. This is burnout. It can cause anxiety, depression, and even physical problems like headaches and migraines. Everyone's situation is different, so there's no one answer for fixing this problem, but yoga can help in several ways.

Yoga helps you learn to relax your mind and body. Yoga lowers stress hormones and increases your production of feel-good endorphins. It improves your sleep quality, and it keeps you flexible, which can help improve your energy levels. Yoga classes are a great way to meet people in an informal setting that's less stressful than a typical social environment.

Fortunately, yoga has been proven to help with mental clarity and concentration — which is why it can be an ideal form of stress relief for someone who experiences burnout from time to time. In this book, you'll learn how to practice yoga for your unique situation so you can finally release all that pent-up tension (and find your balance again).

Yoga

A meditation that uses breathing exercises and physical poses to help you relax and relieve your stress. It's an ancient practice that has been around for thousands of years, and it originated in India (hence its name). You can practice yoga at any fitness level by choosing to focus on a particular type of physical pose or just breathing into your body until you get comfortable with the motions.

Yoga isn't just a bunch of poses that you do in the gym. It's much more than that. Depending on who you ask, there are various definitions for yoga. Here's the one I like best: Yoga is simply the act of paying attention to what is happening in your body and mind right now.

By practicing yoga regularly, you'll become more present - more aware when tension or stress arises, and therefore better able to let it go before it starts causing you pain or discomfort.

Different Types of Yoga

There are many different types of yoga, each with its own goals and benefits. But chances are you already know how yoga's main focus is on meditation. However, different forms of yoga teach you specific poses and breathing techniques to help you deal with different stressors. There are as many as 5,000 yoga types, and we'll be sure to explain the main three major types of yoga below; but first, let's take a look at each type's main focus.

Yoga for Anxiety and Depression: Hatha Yoga

Hatha Yoga focuses primarily on meditation, while Bikram Yoga focuses more on physical poses that target your muscles. These approaches are beneficial for relieving stress but tend to differ in how they approach mental health issues.

Hatha yoga can help relieve stress by helping you better understand your emotions. It's a form of yoga that focuses primarily on meditation and finding peace with yourself and your feelings. Hatha yoga teaches you how to detach from negative emotions by fully experiencing them but ultimately letting them go. It's like holding a crying baby, so you experience all of their feelings, but then handing the baby back to their parents once you're done being upset yourself. Suppose you have anxiety, depression, or some other kind of mental health issue. In that case, hatha yoga might be right for you because it encourages mindfulness and reflection about how you feel emotionally.

Bikram Yoga

On the other hand, Bikram yoga is very physically demanding. It's a form of yoga that includes 26 different poses and two breathing exercises performed in a room that's been heated to 105 degrees. This extreme heat is meant to make you sweat out toxins from your body – including those trapped in your muscles. The heat also opens up your pores so you can better absorb all the minerals and vitamins from the water you drink before and after your session. However, the harsh heat of Bikram yoga has also been shown to raise your body temperature to 105 degrees. Bikram Yoga can cause your blood pressure to increase and make you feel dizzy. It's generally best for people with high blood pressure or dizziness to stick with Hatha Yoga instead.

Hatha Yoga vs. Bikram Yoga

Hatha yoga is a great form of meditation and mental health treatment because it's very calming. It focuses on listening to how you feel inside as you move through various poses that target different areas of your body. Bikram Yoga is a form of yoga that helps relieve stress on your muscles and body while detoxing you at the same time. But it does require a lot of stamina, so it's not recommended for people with conditions like high blood pressure or dizziness.

Yoga for Stress Relief

Vinyasa Yoga isn't designed to treat any mental health conditions. Instead, it's meant to help people who are stressed out from daily life's physical demands. Vinyasa yoga isn't slow or quiet. And rather, it's a kind of yoga that allows your body and mind to become more flexible and aware. It opens up your heart and helps build your strength.

Yoga for Runners

If you have high blood pressure, dizziness, or other health problems that make you feel like you can't do certain poses, then Viniyoga might be off-limits for you. Check out the ViniYoga infographic below to see what poses are safe to do in this form of yoga. You should check with your doctor before trying Vinyasa yoga, especially if you have any back or knee issues.

Unlike other forms of yoga that focus on specific physical poses, Viniyoga is designed for people who are already physically active. It was created by a famous yogi named Shri K. Pattabhi Jois and was originally used to prepare his students for their Ashtanga Yoga practice. Viniyoga helps people become more flexible and relieve them of physical stress like tension in their muscles and joints.

Yoga at home

If you're looking for a yoga method that's very low impact, then Restorative Yoga might be right for you. This form of yoga is designed to help relieve stress in your body and joints while giving you a light stretch at the same time. It's a slow-paced practice that focuses on helping you relax and unwind after a long day. You can do restorative yoga in your home or a quiet, dimly lit space like a bedroom.

If you've been feeling stressed out lately, then it might be time for a yoga retreat. Studies show that mindfulness meditation can help relieve stress better than medication or other treatments. It can also help with mental health conditions like anxiety and depression. So it's a great addition to your wellness routine.

Yoga as part of a workout routine

Yoga is one of the best fitness practices because it helps you understand your body better and work more efficiently with all the different motions you perform. It's the perfect complement to your current workout routine, especially if you're doing an intense cardio workout like Crossfit or Tabata. Research shows that doing cardio and yoga together burns fatter than either activity alone! Yoga helps you get stronger while making it easier for you to find the right amount of rest between each set of exercises.

Benefits of Yoga for burnout

You're more aware of how much stress your body is under every day. When you have that awareness, you can start to take steps to lessen the impact of stress on your overall health and well-being. Yoga is an excellent way to center yourself, relax, and let go of anger, fear, and anxiety when it's not appropriate. A study showed that yoga helps you process the negative emotions associated with burnout! By doing yoga regularly, you can help bring greater clarity and peace to your life.

Besides, yoga's focus on flexibility can help you regain proper posture and movement. When you're in better physical shape, it's easier for your body to handle the demands of stressful situations.

Is Yoga for Burnout right for you?

You might be wondering how yoga for burnout works and if it's an approach that might work for you. As a mental health professional, I specialize in helping people find relief from burnout by teaching them to shift their focus away from stressors that might cause them more harm. This is especially effective with clients dealing with chronic stress or high levels of anxiety or depression. Some are due to their behavior, such as eating too much food or smoking.

Method 4:
Praise Mindfulness Meditation

Mindfulness meditation is a very simple practice. All you need to do is pay attention to what is happening in the present moment. It's a very easy process that anyone can learn! We practice mindfulness meditation by paying attention to thoughts, feelings, and sensations.

When you meditate, your mind becomes. Still, clarity and awareness arise, and you begin to see things in a different light with more compassion for yourself and others, with more ease, with greater balance. You can also meditate in silence just listening to your breath or music.

Why Meditate?

Meditation is very good medicine. Through the practice of meditation, you can learn to connect with your body and mind in new ways, helping you to release physical/emotional tension and experience more balance and calmness. This leads to calmer and more flexible responses in all areas of your life. It also helps you understand where your stress is coming from to choose a healthier response. What has been found is that many people who meditate regularly experience less stress daily; they are less overwhelmed by their daily experiences; they have more peace within themselves; they are generally happier.

Mindfulness Meditation for Burnout

Mindfulness meditation is an effective tool for any person seeking relief from the stress of daily life. But what if burnout is preventing you from benefiting from the practice? As a mindfulness teacher, I have found that many of my students are impeded by stress and anxiety. They are overwhelmed by stress and find it difficult to be present with themselves or others. A considerable number have burnt out in the process. Burnout is a real problem for people who have to cope with severe chronic pain or for caregivers of those who do. We can also get stuck in this cycle of burnout if we don't take steps to address the underlying cause.

I believe that mindfulness meditation can be an important tool for burnout-sufferers. The practice offers a simple yet powerful way to cultivate balance and peace of mind. I've created a sequence of guided mindfulness meditations to help you get started.

Mindfulness Therapy for Burnout

Mindfulness therapy is a form of psychotherapy that also involves meditation practice. In this form of therapy, the therapist guides the client into finding the present moment by focusing on feelings, thoughts, and sensations in one's body and allowing them to let go of negative thoughts and feelings. It is particularly useful as a treatment for anxiety, depression, stress, insomnia, chronic pain – including pain caused by burnout – neurosis, and emotional trauma.

The practice has been shown to help clients gain insight into their feelings and behavior. When people find a way to be in the present moment, they become more aware of their thoughts and actions; therefore, they act more consciously, safely, and skillfully.

Burnout can have far-reaching consequences on health. When we are overwhelmed by stress and overwhelm ourselves with work, we stop taking care of our bodies, eating right, or exercising. We also stop making time for play or pleasure in our lives. Burnout can lead to serious physical diseases such as heart disease and stroke if left unchecked. It can also cause mental confusion that leads to depression, anxiety, or neurotic reactions.

Mindfulness and Burnout

I have found that many of my students are being impeded by stress and anxiety. They are overwhelmed by stress and find it difficult to be present with themselves or others. A considerable number have burnt out in the process. Burnout is a real problem for people who have to cope with severe chronic pain or for caregivers of those who do. We can also get stuck in this cycle of burnout if we don't take steps to address the underlying cause.

Mindfulness meditation offers a method to help us deal with stress, anxiety, and burnout. It is an approach that helps us cultivate awareness, as well as compassion for ourselves and others. I believe that mindfulness meditation can be an important tool for burnout-sufferers. The practice offers a simple yet powerful way to cultivate balance and peace of mind. I've created a sequence of guided mindfulness meditations to help you get started.

1. Becoming aware of the present moment

In this meditation, we focus on the present moment by paying attention to our breathing and become aware of our thoughts, feelings, and sensations. We then bring awareness to how we can be calm in any situation by being mindful of how we feel at any given moment in time.

In this way, we can begin to break free from our overreaction to stressful situations that can lead to burnout. By practicing this meditation regularly, we develop a home base – a feeling of inner peace and clarity that helps us act from wisdom rather than react to anxiety or panic.

2. Finding peace in the heart

Awareness of how we feel is crucial for us to cultivate peace. In this meditation, we allow ourselves to soften into a state of peace. We practice returning to our natural state of calm so that we can find balance in life and at home, at work, with our relationships, and with our friends. We begin to develop an inner calm that helps us take charge of our reactions rather than control them.

3. Becoming aware of pleasure and pain

Once we are aware of how we feel in the present moment, we need to practice developing mindfulness around all aspects of life – pleasure, and pain. In this meditation, we focus on the sensations of pleasure and pain in our bodies. We become aware of how our feelings affect our state of mind by entering into a state of being rather than simply reacting to circumstances. We learn to bring gentleness and stillness into all our relationships.

4. The three characteristics of experience

This meditation gives us guidelines for mindfulness practice in everyday life. We begin by exploring the three characteristics of nature: impermanence, suffering, and non-self: Everything changes; everything comes with attachments or conditions; everything is unfinished, but these three things are not who we are. As we learn to observe these three characteristics, they begin to transform into wisdom in our minds. This gives us the ability to have a sense of stability and kindness in all situations and relationships.

5. Responding with gratitude

In this final meditation, we cultivate a sense of gratitude for all that is good in our lives. We begin to develop an awareness of the miracle of life and our inner resources. We appreciate our friends, family, and ourselves by developing an attitude of kindness toward ourselves and others. In doing so, we begin to cultivate a home base of peace, love, and happiness that gives us the strength to face life's challenges with an open heart and mind.

But how do I get started?

"The answer is simple—show up," says Tarini Nirula, Yoga Teacher and Wellness Advocate. "Worrying about not working out at your present level of ability is the biggest barrier to the practice of yoga." What does that tell you? All you need to do is show up and practice.

Mindfulness meditation is an invaluable tool not only for those of us who can meditate but also for those who find it difficult or too time-consuming. It can be used as a daily reminder that our negative thoughts are not necessarily true, and when our thoughts change, our mood often follows suit. Engaging in mindfulness meditation can help bring us back to the present moment and make it easier to deal with stressors that arise.

The main goal of mindfulness meditation is self-compassion. When we engage in mindfulness meditation, we're not trying to put ourselves down or beat ourselves up; rather, we're trying to create kindness towards ourselves instead of judgment or harsh self-criticism.

Mindfulness meditation is a way to gain self-acceptance and is strongly connected to the benefits of compassion.

To cultivate acceptance, we need to feel safe, and mindfulness practice can help a person feel safe. We often find it hard to express our true feelings and thoughts in face-to-face relationships because of a fear of judgment or rejection, but when we do so through meditation, those fears disappear. We can speak our truth and also hear the truth of others with love rather than fear. In this way, we understand each other better. Through this understanding, we realize that there's no reason not to come together as a community.

Method 5:
Get a Massage

If you are one of the many people who find themselves experiencing the effects of burnout, you might be feeling too exhausted to do anything about it. You may feel like your home is being invaded by an army that just wants to stop you from accomplishing your goals, and this army is getting stronger each day.

That's why I've put together this book all about how massage therapy can help with burnout. We'll talk a little bit about what causes burnout in the first place so that you can try to reverse it before it becomes more than just a headache at the end of a long day. I'll also talk about the signs you might be experiencing burnout, and lastly, I'll talk about all of the ways massage therapy can help with the symptoms of burnout.

Why do you need a massage?

People who have burnout are usually very self-conscious about the fact that they're feeling burnt out and fatigued. If you're feeling burned out, it might feel like everyone can see it, so you might start to avoid social situations and projects because of how much you just want to hide from the world.

Because burnout is so uncomfortable, people usually try to get away from it as quickly as possible. That's why they often put off seeking help when they experience burnout for too long or do horrible things like skip work for days at a time.

If you want to get better, you need to start by addressing the problem rather than trying to ignore it or ignore everyone around you. When you get a massage for burnout, your massage therapist will listen to you and help you understand what's going on in your life with burnout.

Sometimes all it takes is being heard out and having someone point out the symptoms of burnout that are right in front of your face. Once your massage therapist knows what's wrong with you, they can teach you how massage can help with your burnout symptoms.

Benefits of massage for burnout

Massage therapy is an ancient healing art that has changed a lot since it was first developed over 2,000 years ago. The benefits of massage could not be better for you right now than they are at this moment.

When you go for a massage for burnout, your therapist will be able to evaluate the source of your burnout and figure out how they can help you get better. Getting a master's degree in massage therapy will give you the kind of hands-on training that will enable you to get back into work so fast that no one would ever suspect what's going on in your life.

A therapist should evaluate whether a specific massage technique is a right technique to use on you. They should also figure out how you prefer your massage to feel, and they should know exactly the right pressure that you need for the exact length of time that it takes to heal your burnout.

The benefits of massage are enormous during this stage of burnout. You'll get the healing effects of the Swedish technique, but if you're a sports enthusiast, you'll get all of the added benefits of a deep tissue massage. Massage was developed as a healing art for certain people, and now it's ready to help everyone.

Benefits for the body

When you get a massage for burnout, you'll experience major benefits around the muscle and nerve fiber level. When your muscles are tight, it's hard to move your body, and it becomes more difficult to think about what to do. This is a common effect of burnout because most people cannot function correctly or get their tasks done. But when you get a massage for burnout, you'll be able to relax all of your muscles and work towards your goals with fresh energy. You'll also start to feel like you move better with your body instead of feeling like some other force controls it. Relaxation is the best way to feel empowered, and that's what you'll get from a massage for burnout.

The benefits of massage therapy for burnout are so great because massage therapy can help you stay better and do more in your life. You'll be able to live more freely every day, but it won't hurt your pocketbook one bit. Massage therapy is already one of the most popular types of treatments around, and the benefits for you will be even greater than that.

Massage therapy will also help improve circulation in parts of your body that are overworked and tired. If you have poor circulation, your muscles will be tired and sore after long periods of hard work. The benefits of massage therapy will lessen the severity of these problems so that you can work out again for longer periods without getting tired or sore as fast as you normally would.

The benefits to the mind

Massage therapy can also greatly improve those symptoms that are associated with physician burnout. A massage therapist could help find the source of your symptoms and get rid of it before it gets worse. The effects on the mind and body from a massage will decrease stress, improve coordination and balance, promote relaxation, relieve anxiety, and most importantly, cure burnout.

Some of the real benefits of massage therapy:

- Improved overall health
- Enhanced mood and mental state
- Raised energy levels
- Increased circulation and blood flow
- Reduction of muscle and joint pain
- Increased mental acuity
- Prevention of fatigue and burnout

Because the benefits of a massage are so great for burnout, it's no surprise that they will all be there as soon as you get back to work. You'll be able to work smarter, faster, and better while having more energy. You won't feel exhausted or drained from doing more, which is why a massage is such a fantastic solution for your burnout. Your therapist can determine precisely what kind of massage is right for you and how long you should have it, depending on your situation.

So, now that you know about burnout massage and why it is important for your health, you can now be proactive in preventing this condition.

You should speak to a massage therapist today if you have the symptoms of burnout so they can recommend this service. When used appropriately, burnout massage reduces symptoms of stress and burnout and increases sleep quality and productivity.

Method 6:
Practice Art Therapy

If you find yourself feeling as if you are mentally and physically exhausted but unable to stop working or take a break, then chances are you're suffering from burnout. Many different factors can spur burnout, so why not try practicing some art therapy? This creative outlet is a fantastic way to wind down from the stresses of everyday life and work while also allowing your brain to think up new ideas.

Art Therapy

Also known as psychotherapy with art, this therapeutic method was originally pioneered by the French writer and psychologist Jean Antoine Fabre-Vernon in the 19th Century. It involves communicating feelings and thoughts through different artistic media, such as painting or drawing. This allows one to release distressing emotions and reclaim control of their mental well-being.

The process of art therapy helps you to gain awareness of your feelings and will also show you what you're feeling more concretely and tangibly than just words on a page. It's a way to channel your thoughts and feelings into something tangible, either drawing, painting, or sculpting. The medium allows you to understand better how you're feeling, allowing for a healthier state of mind in the long run.

Creative Ways to Deal with Burnout

Write journaling is a fantastic way to take the weight off your shoulders and express what you're feeling. You can write about anything that is bothering you or even use the notes as a springboard to brainstorm brainstorms for future projects. It will help you gain perspective on how you're feeling and could also be used as a personal diary in the long run.

Paint watercolors

If you're feeling too exhausted to sit down and write, watercolor is a great way to blow off some steam. It's a quick and easy process that allows you to express your thoughts and feelings in a simple yet powerful manner.

Start sculpting!

Sculpting is a fantastic way to let your imagination run wild — it doesn't matter if you have no previous experience or not, as most of the hard work will be done by your hands. Just make sure you take your time with the process, taking your time to think about what you want to create.

Go for a walk

Even if just for a few minutes, a short walk is a perfect way to clear your head. Not only does it help circulate the blood and cleanse your nerves, but it also gives you the chance to think up new ideas and visualize them in real life!

Draw

If you prefer to keep your hands moving, drawing is another great way to let your creativity run wild. Some people also find it easier to express their feelings through drawings — so try it out and see if this works for you.

Cook up a storm in the kitchen!

Cooking is an incredibly therapeutic experience that allows you to take your mind off things for a little while. Plus, it's a great way to express your creativity, especially if you're the type to add your twist to dishes!

Compose a piece of music

If you're familiar with musical instruments or singing, then why not try composing your song? You can either perform it yourself or upload it online for other people to hear and enjoy. Composition is an excellent way to blow off steam and let go of some built-up emotions.

Take a walk around the block

Ever noticed that your mind wanders a lot when you're alone? It's a great way to clear your head, letting your thoughts go where they need to and inspiring you with fresh ideas.

Model

This method is especially useful for those with an artistic flair. Just take a moment to imagine yourself posing in front of school children or perhaps in front of a group of people you don't know. This is a fantastic way to practice your improvisational skills and show off your creative sides.

Make some origami

Origami is a great way to take your mind off things, as well as being incredibly fun! It's a simple form of art that can be made using paper. You can make people or animals by folding pieces of paper into different shapes, or you can even create larger pieces like a whole bird!

Go nuts

If you're feeling particularly creative, why not make a collage out of your old artworks? You can either use pictures and other art forms to do yourself or use pieces from magazines and newspapers. This is a great way to get inspired by things that you have already created or done, and it's also a fantastic way to show off your skills.

Draw or paint one of your favorite characters

One way to express yourself is by drawing or painting one of your favorite characters. You can even draw them from a story that you've written, or you can even create new characters from scratch! This is a great creative process that will help you think up new ideas and let out your inner child.

Write down your goals

This is something you should do daily, but it's especially important when you're feeling burned out. Make a list of all the things you want to accomplish in life. It could be as simple as visiting a certain place or finishing your favorite book, but make sure that it's something that will make you happy.

Explore your artistic side by painting on canvas

You can use any type of paintbrush or even your fingers to create the artworks, and they don't have to be perfect! This process will help you interestingly express yourself and help take off some stress. After all, this is supposed to be fun!

Read a book by yourself

This is another excellent way to let your mind wander. You can find a good book about something that you are interested in, or you can even pick up one of your own as it will make reading more enjoyable and interesting! This is a great way to reflect on the events of the day and relax.

Look through your old photos

You can take a trip down memory lane by looking through some of the old pictures you have taken. Notice how you looked at different stages in your life and how you've changed over the years. This is a chance to reflect on the journey we've been on so far, and it's an excellent way to reminisce and smile.

Create a scrapbook

This is something that you should do once a year, or even more often if you like. A scrapbook can be used to document anything from memories to your childhood and even your work. It's a great way to share the moments that you think are important, and it's worth investing some time in something like this!

Art Therapy and Burnout

These are just a handful of things you can do to keep your mind in an open and positive place. When you release all of the toxins from your body, you will move forward more positively.

Remember: do whatever it takes to get through this! It's okay if you decide that your old ways were better. You can always go back to them later if you want, but don't let burnout rule over your life. You have to be in control and be positive, even when you feel as though you're alone.

If you struggle immensely with burnout, it may be time to see a therapist and get yourself out of the battle zone and back into a positive place. Your life is your own; it can't help but be better if you continue to let it burn out. So get up! Breakthrough the barrier! Do something! Your life will not improve until you do.

Art Therapy Benefits

Acceptance and compassion

Helps you nurture yourself and others

Aids in self-understanding and personal growth

Builds communication skills

Stimulates imagination, thinking, problem-solving, decision making, creativity, and more.

Method 7:
Try acupuncture

Acupuncture is the practice of inserting thin needles into your skin at certain points along meridians aligned with bodily organs, glands, and tissues. The insertion of these needles stimulates points on the meridians, which is believed to promote healing. Some immediate benefits: acupuncture can relieve pain, reduce nausea from chemotherapy treatments, improve fertility rates in women who have been trying unsuccessfully for a year or more to become pregnant, lift moods and alleviate anxiety. All acupuncture treatments involve needle placement on specific body areas according to an individual's health needs.

Does Acupuncture Work for Stress and Burnout?

Many people who try acupuncture say that it helps them cope with stress and burnout, but how does it work? Changes have been observed in the human body when acupuncture is applied to the skin. In particular, there are changes in hormone levels and the autonomic nervous system. It appears that when someone receives acupuncture, endorphins are released throughout their body, and they feel relaxed because of the increase in oxytocin levels. All of these changes contribute towards stress reduction that people often experience with acupuncture treatments.

Acupuncture and Burnout

Burnout is characterized by an overwhelming feeling of depletion and negativity. Some therapists and psychiatrists believe that burnout is the result of too much stress in someone's life. These doctors encourage their patients to practice self-care to alleviate symptoms of burnout, including eating right, sleeping well, joining support groups, practicing mindfulness, and doing things that promote a sense of meaning and purpose.

Acupuncture is a type of therapy that is closely related to traditional Chinese medicine. It has been practiced in China for thousands of years and is based on the theory that there are channels through which qi flows. Qi, also known as chi, is the energy or life force that animates living beings. These channels are called meridians and are part of what Chinese Medicine refers to as the microcosmic system. This system consists of a large network of channels that flow with energy, including everything from your organs to glands and other tissues and structures in your body. Every organ, gland, and tissue has its meridian in this system.

Acupuncture may be one tool that individuals use to lessen burnout because it can help them naturally cope with stress. It also helps patients with anxiety by addressing the underlying causes to no longer feel anxious or worried about certain things.

Asking for Acupuncture

Even though there are many benefits associated with acupuncture, some people who have tried it say that they find it challenging to receive treatments. If you're struggling with the process, you can always ask your acupuncturist for help. In addition to asking your acupuncturist for advice on how to feel more comfortable during treatments, there are also a few steps that you can take on your own:

Be prepared for treatments: Because most people feel relaxed when they receive acupuncture, some will naturally fall asleep during their sessions. If you are someone who struggles with this, you will need to prepare for your treatments by avoiding caffeine and ensuring that you have an empty bladder.

Consider what you want to achieve: Many people who seek acupuncture treatments do so because it helps them feel relaxed and less stressed. However, if you want a more targeted experience, there are ways that you can focus your sessions on the specific areas of your body where you're feeling pain or discomfort. For instance, if you are trying to relieve back pain or migraine headaches, the acupuncturist will use needles in points along the meridians that travel from the head to the feet to undo imbalances in your body.

Encourage the acupuncturist: Before you start your sessions, it is important to make sure that you are listening to your acupuncturist's instructions. This is because they will not only give you specific instructions on how to position yourself during your treatments, but they will also help you determine the most effective points for acupuncture.

Relax as much as possible: Before entering the acupuncture room, always take a few deep breaths and count to ten if it helps you relax. It's also advisable that you put on comfortable clothing that is loose and breathable so that the needles don't cause any discomfort or pain. Take care of yourself after your acupuncture sessions, take the time to eat a big meal, and get plenty of sleep every night. Your body needs this extra care to feel restored and replenished after the treatment.

Keep up with what your acupuncturist recommends: When you walk out of your first session, don't assume that your acupuncturist will call you back if you need additional treatments in the future. It's up to you to make sure that they know how much you appreciate their services.

Say thank you: To ensure you can take advantage of all the benefits of acupuncture, you salways give your acupuncturist a sincere thank you. If they have helped you completely feel better, make sure that they know how much their services meant to you.

Consider the Frequency of Treatments: When it comes to getting acupuncture treatments, it's important to consider how frequently these are needed to reduce stress and burnout symptoms effectively. Since there is research suggesting that acupuncture can work best when used every few days, it might be best to stick with this schedule if possible.

Benefits of Acupuncture: according to research, acupuncture has been found to help relieve stress and burnout symptoms. One of the major benefits of acupuncture is that it seems to increase physical pain tolerance. This is particularly helpful for people trying to deal with the symptoms of burnout as they often feel extremely exhausted and in a lot of pain.

Acupuncture is also thought to prevent people from feeling frustrated or overwhelmed, which can often cause them to lash out at their loved ones.

There is also evidence suggesting that acupuncture can help boost positive emotions, which is helpful for those who struggle with feeling hopeless or depressed after dealing with burnout-related symptoms.

A great part of the success of acupuncture seems to be its ability to help people relax and unwind. For example, research has shown that the more stressed people feel after a stressful situation, 's more likely for they to suffer from insomnia. Thus, it seems as though relaxing as much as possible can reduce the symptoms associated with burnout and reduce stress.

Over time, practicing acupuncture can also reduce many conditions linked with stress and burnout, including migraines and even heart disease. One study found that getting acupuncture treatment for migraines reduced the symptoms by 71% over two weeks.

Another study has also shown an extremely strong link between acupuncture and the reduction of stress. This study also found that participants experienced an 86% reduction in stress after having done the treatment for two weeks.

The Chinese have been using this treatment method for thousands of years, and since everything is connected, this seems to be a very effective yet safe way of helping people with stress and burnout symptoms.

Acupuncture can be a great way to relieve stress and burnout symptoms for many people, but there are certain things to keep in mind before trying it out.

Method 8:
Exercise

No question working out is a great way to relieve stress. Still, for people who are already experiencing burnout - stress, exhaustion, and tiredness from excessive work or an unstable job – there can be a risk in overdoing it. The key to finding the right balance is finding ways to maintain your mental health while also taking care of your physical needs. If you're experiencing burnout or you feel like you need to take time for yourself, check out these tips on how to find balance in your life:

- Exercise regularly for at least 150 minutes each week

- Get enough sleep

- Reduce the amount of time you spend in front of a screen (TV, computer, etc.)

- Schedule time for fun activities or take some time off from work

- Focus on good work habits, such as avoiding multitasking and setting realistic goals

- Eat balanced meals and snack at regular intervals

- Get involved in a community or social activity.

You may also be interested to hear about these three quick and easy strategies to help you relax:

· Stretch regularly throughout the day. When you're tense, your muscles get tighter and tighter until they feel like they're ready to burst! Regular stretching can help ease muscle tension, encourage blood flow, and improve mobility and flexibility.

· Yoga can help to improve your flexibility and strength. If you don't have time for a full yoga session, doing a few simple stretches such as lunges, squats, or standing forward bends can help minimize tightness and tension in the body. You can do them regularly throughout the day or as you're driving or waiting in line at the grocery store!

· Mindfulness meditation is another great way to relax. This is a meditation technique that helps you bring your attention back to the present moment. Research has shown that mindfulness meditation reduces stress and improves sleep quality by promoting relaxation and improving breathing patterns. You can practice mindfulness meditation on your own, or you can enlist the help of a meditation instructor to help you improve your technique.

Why Exercise?

Exercising can help you achieve a better work-life balance because it promotes good health, reduces anxiety and depression, helps with weight loss, improves energy levels, boosts productivity and self-esteem, and helps keep you younger-looking for longer.

After work, many people struggle to find time for exercise. Regular exercise is one of the best things you can do for yourself when it comes to burnout. A recent study found that increased levels of physical activity were strongly related to lower levels of burnout. Participants who did not engage in as much physical activity had higher levels of emotional exhaustion and depersonalization and lower feelings of personal accomplishment and professional efficacy.

Aerobic Exercise (Level 1/Low Intensity)

Low-intensity aerobic exercises can help relieve the stress caused by burnout, increase your energy levels, give you more emotional balance and help you sleep better at night. Aerobic exercise may also help you lose weight, or if you're already carrying excess weight, it can help you burn calories. To effectively relieve burnout, at least 30 minutes of aerobic activity three to four times a week is recommended.

Active recovery (Level 2/Moderate Intensity)

Active recovery is when your body moves while resting. This type of exercise helps improve your strength and balance and can be practiced as aerobic and anaerobic exercises. Active recovery is particularly effective for reducing muscle tightness and improving flexibility (also known as range-of-motion). It is recommended that active recovery should take place three to four times per week for 15-20 minutes each time.

Physical activity breaks (Level 3/High Intensity)

When you are experiencing burnout, a physical activity break can help to reduce fatigue, improve alertness and concentration, and enhance motivation. Taking a five-minute walk outdoors or a five-minute exercise break at work every hour can help you return to work with more energy.

Before you exercise...

The first thing you should do before starting an exercise program is to check with your doctor. If you have any medical conditions, allergies, or other factors that may make it unsafe for you to begin an exercise program, be sure to talk about it with your doctor.

Body awareness and relaxation

Body awareness refers to the ability of the mind to perceive and interpret sensory information from the body. Relaxation is when our bodies undergo changes in physiological activity that are opposite of the stress response. Two basic components can define relaxation: 1) Body awareness 2) Physical relaxation. Both components are important for reducing stress levels, but it is important to note that physical relaxation alone is not enough for improving health. A relaxation response can be induced by meditation, progressive muscle relaxation, Yoga, etc.

Exercise is awesome. Just ask anyone who's ever "just done a little bit of walking" or stretched their arms. It'll make you feel healthier, happier, more alert, and alive than you felt before. And while it might seem strange to take up a hobby with the explicit goal of pushing your body to its limits to improve its health, the benefits are seriously worth it. So go on, see if you can manage to exercise today. And let me know how you get on. Cheers!

However, sometimes we don't use exercise to improve our health. We use it to distract us from our problems and help us forget about them.

If you're feeling frustrated by limitations induced by stress or other mental health issues — and not just one day here and there, but days on end — then exercise is something that can help get things back on track. Exercise helps with your mental health in a few ways. First off, it improves your physical health. Secondly, it can reduce stress and help you destress. And thirdly, it's an outlet for pent-up energy or frustration.

In a more general sense, exercise is just awesome. It makes you feel good about yourself – and we could all use more of that.

Method 9:
Cut Down on Caffeine Consumption

We've heard the caffeine buzz, but it's time to bring you back down to earth. Maybe some of us are completely dependent on coffee and need a few extra cups per day to get through our morning routine, or maybe we're just wondering if we can drink less and still be on our A-game.

You're probably well aware of the dangers of high caffeine consumption, but ever wonder why? Caffeine can cause a host of side effects, including anxiety, insomnia, and irritability. They may seem like fairly minor inconveniences to you now, but it won't be long before these side effects begin to affect your relationships with friends and family. It's not worth it! Cut down on your caffeine consumption today.

A cup of coffee or tea isn't going to kill you. Its natural caffeine will give you a little boost in the morning, but if you keep drinking it each day, it's just going to build up and give you a headache. Pack away your daily cup of coffee or tea and switch over to decaf. Decaf drinkers are less likely to suffer from insomnia and anxiety than those who drink regular coffee. Switching over can benefit your overall health since the effects that caffeine has on the brain are still present in decaf products.

What is Caffeine?

Caffeine is a naturally occurring stimulant found in certain plants, seeds, and nuts. It's not the same as coffee, tea, or chocolate, but most of us know what it is by its "in-yer-face" buzz. Energy drinks can contain up to 200 milligrams of caffeine per serving. This is more than twice the amount found in a Starbucks coffee (80 mg per cup).

How does caffeine work? This is a "drug" that acts as a stimulant in the brain. It works by blocking adenosine, a brain chemical that slows down neuron activity. The extra speed makes you feel more awake and alert. By blocking adenosine, caffeine allows dopamine and norepinephrine to move more freely throughout the body resulting in feelings of increased energy and alertness, elevated moods, and enhanced concentration.

Caffeine is naturally found in coffee, tea, cola, chocolate, and energy drinks which vary in the amount of caffeine they contain. Coffee has been shown to have a variety of health benefits. It's a great source of antioxidants, contains natural calcium and magnesium, and offers a high level of vitamins B2 (riboflavin), B6 (pyridoxine), C (ascorbic acid), iron, potassium, and zinc. But drinking too much coffee or other caffeinated products can lead to dependence or addiction.

What is caffeine withdrawal? Caffeine withdrawal occurs after you stop consuming caffeine for some time.

Health Concerns

Caffeine has been associated with insomnia, anxiety, and nervousness. It can also cause headaches, fast heart rate, indigestion, and even increased blood pressure. Caffeine has been linked to cardiovascular diseases, including high blood pressure, heart attack, and stroke.

Caffeine has become a popular ingredient in energy drinks like Red Bull and Monster. Energy drinks have been subject to numerous health concerns, including over-consumption by athletes (athletes using energy drinks are at an increased risk for dehydration) and an association with long-term effects of depression and suicide.

Athletes have stopped taking caffeine because it makes them susceptible to muscle cramps after strenuous exercise. Even though these products boast gains in strength and endurance, studies show that they do not enhance athletic performance.

Caffeine and Burnout

The psychological effects of caffeine can significantly impact your ability to perform at your best consistently. Unfortunately, there is no magic pill that can help overcome these issues, but you can take some easy steps to help ease the burden. These tips may not be fool-proof, but they're even better than popping an energy drink that could potentially do more harm than good!

1. Reduce your caffeine intake by 200 mg each day until you reach a more acceptable level.

Sometimes, we turn to our caffeinated beverages as the source of energy we need to get through our long days when a little bit of exercise would go a lot further. There's nothing wrong with enjoying a tall cup of delicious Joe, and there's nothing wrong with using it as a substitute for physical activity either, but you have to be careful not to rely on it too much. If you have the option, try to incorporate physical activity into your daily routine instead of relying on caffeine for energy and inspiration! It is much healthier this way and will have more lasting effects!

2. Be prepared for decreased athletic performance.

Especially for those who enjoy participating in intense exercises, caffeine could be considered a necessary evil. Even though you may be used to that extra boost that a cup of coffee gives you during your workout, you have to be careful not to rely on it too much. Be prepared if your athletic performance will decline as a result of cutting back! If you're going to exercise, do it when you're most rested and make an effort to get your exercise over with as soon as possible so that you can go about the rest of your day without depending on caffeine.

3. Consume caffeine in moderation.

Most of us may be more used to caffeine than you'd think, but for most people, there's a threshold beyond which they can no longer tolerate the energy boost and side effects, such as upset stomachs or jitters. Just like alcohol, over-consumption can have negative effects on your physical health. Be sure to stick within your limits so that you don't have to contend with negative side effects!

4. Watch out for hidden caffeine sources.

We use caffeine in so many different ways that we don't even realize that it could be found in many of our favorite foods. If you eat food products containing a lot of caffeine, you may not have even realized that you're potentially getting more caffeine than you bargained for. There are even some items that contain only trace amounts of the substance, so clearing out your cupboards and kitchen cabinets will help reduce your caffeine intake. Besides, be sure to check ingredient labels and try to avoid any foods containing "naturally occurring caffeine" if at all possible.

5. Limit caffeinated beverages.

There's nothing wrong with drinking a cup of coffee on the weekends, but try to limit your intake to that one time and don't treat it as a reward for working hard all week. Remember that just like any other addictive substance, caffeine can eventually cause dependence. And we've heard the caffeine buzz, so we know who's most likely to become dependent on caffeine.

6. Drink decaffeinated coffee if you can't kick the habit.

Suppose you're going to be unable to kick the habit, at least attempt to wean yourself slowly. You can still get your caffeine fix without consuming as much of it. The more you drink, the less caffeine will be needed to provide you with the same level of energy and alertness. There are some interesting studies out there stating that you might be able to reduce your withdrawal symptoms by consuming decaffeinated coffee instead of caffeinated beans.

The Effects of Caffeine on the Brain

Our brains are made up of a series of interconnected networks. As we interact with the world around us, send and receive messages from others, and make decisions, these networks allow us to respond appropriately. This means that it can disrupt one or more parts of this network when caffeine is introduced to the system. This will affect how we function as human beings. Caffeine affects different parts of the brain in specific ways and can cause some severe side effects.

The relationship between caffeine, the brain, and behavior is the foundation of modern neuroscience. When researchers began to study caffeine regulation in the 1920s, they focused on how it affected blood pressure and heart rate. Since that time, we've learned a lot about how caffeine affects the brain and body.

Much of this information came from animals in which scientists had infused caffeine directly into their nervous systems. These studies contributed to developing a theory known as "the central nervous system theory of action." This theory argues that drug action is initiated at the level of the brain and works its way throughout nerves in other parts of the body.

It is believed that caffeine acts as a stimulant on the brain, so caffeine does not usually cause any problems for most people when they ingest it in moderation.

Bad Effects of Too Much Caffeine

A lot of people love having a cup of coffee in the morning, but when you drink too much of it in a short amount of time, you'll begin to experience side effects including:

1. Headaches
2. Irritability
3. Anxiety attacks, panic attacks, and depression.

Bad Habits of Taking Caffeine

1. Consuming too much caffeine can lead to addiction.
2. Caffeine can increase your heart rate.
3. It will keep you up at night if you consume too much caffeine.

Caffeine is a drug found naturally in coffee and chocolate. However, most of the caffeine that we ingest comes from soda beverages.

Caffeine Alternatives

1) Tea

2) Chocolate

3) Caffeine pills

4) Caffeine powder

5) Energy drinks

6) Soda pop

The caffeine buzz is a lie. It's probably a sad excuse to keep you from getting things done.

Method 10:
Rest when on Leave

We all get burned out at some point in our lives. It's just a natural part of life. Not all burnouts are created equally, and some can lead to more serious problems. If you're going on leave from your job, it might seem like the perfect time to get that much-needed rest. But in reality, extended periods of inactivity can lead to a sluggish immune system and other health problems. Instead of just chilling out and waiting for days to pass, try these tips on how to stay active while taking a break from work:

1. Keep moving with any type of physical activity you enjoy - even brisk walking counts!
2. Drop by your favorite cafe for a chat or reading session with friends.
3. Set up an imaginary treasure hunt for kids in the neighborhood as they face off against each other and hunt for clues.

Rest to Prevent Burnout

There are many health benefits to staying active, and most of us already know that burnout is bad for our well-being. It may also reduce their chances of injury or work-related illnesses if they do get injured or sick.

But let's face it, being tired is inevitable. Unless you're working a bunch of physically demanding jobs, you're probably going to feel like you've been run over by a truck at some point during the day. So if burnout is an issue for you, don't worry! There are a few things that can help prevent burnout from getting out of hand.

1. Take breaks - more than likely, your boss already does this.
2. Being active - even just walking around every day will help you avoid burnout and increase your energy levels.
3. Take time to enjoy the scenery. It's nice to visit places in your neighborhood (maybe while on break) and just take in how beautiful it is.
4. Have friends over for dinner so you can reconnect and spend some quality time with them. They're real people who care about you, even if they don't always realize it!
5. Maintain good sleep habits (see below). A lack of quality sleep often causes burnout. Sleep is just as important as food when it comes to staying healthy.
6. Remember to take your medications as prescribed. They're there to help you-- and they'll do their job best if you use them.

How to get a good night's rest

1. When you go to bed, make sure you're reading something that will stimulate your brain but isn't too difficult (in case you have trouble sleeping). Maybe even try some guided meditation or relaxation exercises before going to sleep.
2. Limit your use of electronics before bed, or keep them well out of sight to avoid distractions; they make it harder to fall asleep.

3. Use headphones to cut out the noise outside your room. Try a white noise machine for a quieter environment.

4. If you have trouble falling asleep, try this tip: Get up earlier in the morning and do any activity that gets your blood pumping good and early-- like goes for a walk or even plays some soccer with the kids!

Some people simply can't handle not being at work all day long-- others prefer it that way.

Strategies to Help You Rest from Burnout

· Go for a walk. Walk the dogs. Walk around the neighborhood. Get some air, put your feet on the ground, and enjoy being alive!

· Take a class or participate in a workshop to expand your knowledge in an area you're passionate about. Enroll yourself in an art class or creative writing workshop or maybe something like basic computer programming classes? The sky's the limit with this one! If you have kids, arrange for them to take part as well-- this could be a great bonding experience for all of you!

· Prepare meals and freeze them for those days when you're too tired to cook.

· Join a club that would allow you to catch up on your social life without having to be tied down to specific hours.

Benefits of resting

Resting is an important part of your body's recovery process. The human body needs a period to rest from its normal functions to recover properly, and the brain has a similar function.

A healthy body keeps on functioning normally even after long periods of inactivity. For example, resting muscles are still capable of controlling heartbeat and breathing, even if you are sleeping for days at a time, provided you maintain basic hydration levels throughout this time.

If your body is feeling good enough to perform daily chores like walking and carrying suitcases (and it's not hurting too much), there isn't much reason to have exceptions made to this rule.

When you take time off, you're doing yourself and the people around you a favor. If you are burnt out, taking a few days off may just be what the doctor ordered. It can also act as a wake-up call and help your body start functioning better again.

An opportunity to relax for some time can be an effective treatment for burnout symptoms. The body needs rest and recovery time, so getting this kind of mental break can give it needed rest and much-needed energy.

This can also be a great time to take stock and see what needs to be addressed. It might change your perspective on whether or not you need to take a step back or if you should make a bold move.

It may also help you reorganize your priorities in life. If you cannot take a break from work during the holidays, maybe you should take some time off now to be refreshed by the time the holiday season comes. You might find that a little extra energy can go a long way.

Finally, this can also help eliminate some of the frustrations that may be building up inside you. You'll come back refreshed and ready to handle your day-to-day challenges.

Method 11:
Set Boundaries

Life is full of interruptions, distractions, and meltdowns. It's difficult to focus and get things done when you can't say no or your time is constantly interrupted. Turn off your phone. You already know that you use your phone too much, but do you know how much impact it has on you? Downtime is essential because it allows us to process information and reset without distraction. If you need help with this, put your phone in another room or note where you will see it to remind yourself not to check your phone.

Shut down social media. Unless you run a business that requires you to be on social media regularly, it is not a good idea to be on it all day long. Whenever I want to get focused and have some downtime, I turn off my phone and shut down my social media.

Minimize your Google searches. Google is an amazing tool for research and finding information fast but if you don't need it right now, turn it off. If you need to find something later on, then look it up when you are doing something productive instead of wasting time by looking at your phone in the middle of the night trying to find something that can wait until morning.

Avoid impromptu meetings. They are tempting, but they are distracting. If you know that a person stops by unexpectedly, be prepared with something to do or a stand-up meeting plan beforehand, so you don't feel like you need to have a meeting in the middle of the workday.

Identify your distractions and eliminate them from your day. If you know that someone will interrupt, then identify where your interruption will come from and plan for it before it happens. When I am on the hook to do things at home, I check in with my kids before leaving if they want my help. If I know that after work, I will meet with someone again, then make sure everything is organized and ready beforehand.

Stay focused when you need to leave the office. If you know that you have an important deadline coming up and need all your energy to get it done, then set boundaries. If your wife reminds you that she needs some help cleaning after work, remind her that they can discuss it another time because you have to get home and finish those last few things.

Keep distractions out of your work location. When I'm at the office, I keep interruptions out of my workspace. My office is only used for work, so I shouldn't be getting phone calls or texts in there, and if my meetings are going to be in here, then make sure people know they cannot stop by unexpectedly.

Be prepared for potential interruptions. If I know that a meeting is coming up, I make sure to put my phone in airplane mode because it will distract me from somewhere and talk on my phone. If I have something that needs to get done that day, leave it in my bag so if an interruption comes up that day, I can do it afterward.

Turn off your notifications. When you are trying to stay focused, turn off notifications to keep yourself from being interrupted all of the time. Plus, when you don't have anything you need to respond to them, it takes less time and will help with your productivity in the long run.

Boundaries and Burnout

It's important to set boundaries to stay focused and get the most out of your workday. If you don't set boundaries, there will be way too many distractions and interruptions that prevent you from getting anything done. Not only do you need to set boundaries with distractions and interruptions, but you also need to set them for social media. I know it's tempting to check Twitter and Facebook when you are supposed to be working, but not only is it distracting, but if you spend too much time on social media, you are burning yourself out and getting less work done in the long run.

You have to protect your time if you want to be productive in the long run. If you don't have the energy, then end your workday early and go home. If dealing with an interruption is going to be too much, don't deal with it while trying to get work done.

By setting boundaries, you can give yourself time to get back on track, so now let's talk about what happens when we break them. If we give in to all of our distractions and break our boundaries every day, we will burn out quickly. It's only natural for us to break these rules from time to time, but the key is how we respond when that happens. It's important to remember that when we break our boundaries, we need to remember to bite the bullet and get back on track because we would fall even further behind if we didn't.

The first step in burnout is when we feel the urge to give in. This can happen any time of the day, especially when you feel like you can't take another minute of work. When this happens, it may help to remind yourself that it isn't worth sacrificing your health or well-being for work during these times. It may also help if you try and turn down tempting requests because sometimes they are unnecessary distractions from what you need to accomplish.

Another step is when we procrastinate. As I said earlier, it's only natural for us to do this, but it is important to recognize a problem and then change. It may help give yourself some deadlines to know when you have to get something done to manage your time better.

The last step in burnout is when we make up excuses for why we aren't getting work done. This should be the step where you realize that everything that happened before couldn't be helped, and all the things in life aren't going to stop happening if you can accomplish what you need during this time of stress.

How to draw boundaries

Setting boundaries is not something that happens overnight, but there are some things you can do to help yourself along the way. First, it may be helpful to use an electronic checklist so you don't forget to do anything. You can also use a notepad or sticky notes and put things like "accountant tomorrow" on one side and your daily goals on the other.

The key is to keep these things easily accessible and show yourself how easily you could accomplish them if you just give it a try. For example, if your list says, "call your bookkeeper tomorrow," start calling her right now because she won't remember tomorrow.

Another way to make boundaries for yourself is by setting goals for a certain amount of time and then when you complete them treating yourself. This is a great way to reward yourself for a job well done because it will make you look forward to more work.

Finally, if you need to try something new, always go ahead and try. You can always decide that you don't like it later on, but sometimes trying is the only way to find out if something works.

Once you set a boundary, hold firm

To begin with, you should try to set mini-goals for yourself. After you complete these goals, reward yourself. This will make it easier to complete the next tasks because you've already been rewarded and can look forward to more.

Also, check in now and then to see how far you've come instead of constantly looking at the result. If you feel like you're falling behind or that things are not working out well, take a step back and ask someone what they think about what is going on or if they know why things have changed since the last time things were going well.

If you feel like things are not working out well, then take a step back and ask someone what they think about what is going on or if they know why things have changed since the last time things were going well. If you do not get any joy out of what you are doing, this can make you very unhappy.

If you do not get any joy out of what you are doing, this can make you very unhappy. Sometimes trying to impress people is the only thing that we have going for us.

Sometimes trying to impress people is the only thing that we have going for us. You will be amazed at how little things make a big difference when it comes to your happiness.

You will be amazed at how little things make a big difference in your happiness in life.

Finally, otherwise, just give up. It is hard to do but sometimes doing certain things isn't worth the effort. You can still be happy while doing other activities so long as they don't interfere with your life goals.

We all need boundaries sometimes. We often don't like to set them because it means we are admitting defeat or giving up. Try setting boundaries with your work or with your friends to be successful in the long term.

We all want to be the best parent, partners, and friends we can be. But sometimes it's hard. It's hard not to get angry when your daughter doesn't stop playing outside with her friends so you can bathe her, or it's hard not to snap at your partner when they forget about dinner again. But it's important that when you feel frustrated, you don't act on it. It's important that you set boundaries and stick to them. The first step is awareness – being aware of why you're stressed and what situations bring it out. Remind yourself that your children are not to blame for your feelings, and understand that sometimes other people are just frustrating! Next, take a deep breath, make a plan, and stick to it. Don't let people push your buttons! If they do, acknowledge their behavior without negatively engaging with them. And lastly, remember: You are not alone! Others feel the same way as you do.

As a parent, it can be hard to set boundaries and stick to them. It's easy to lash out at your children for things they do or just feel angry and frustrated when you don't get what you want. But remember: They are not responsible for your feelings. It helps if you set clear boundaries with your children about what you will and won't accept.

It's important that these boundaries are clear, but also that the outcome is fair. Don't expect too much of your child right from the start, but make sure that they know exactly what is expected of them and how they can improve their behavior.

Setting boundaries is one of the most important skills you'll learn as a parent and as an adult in general; these boundaries will help make sure that everyone in your life knows what you're willing to do for them and what you're not willing to do for them.

Method 12:
Practice Self-compassion

Self-compassion is the act of treating oneself with kindness. It's a way of caring about oneself when one has been struggling. Being self-compassionate is not the same as being self-indulgent and may even be tough love at times. Self-compassion is not a sign of weakness. It's a sign of strength. If we are to be kind to ourselves, then we will need the same kindness from others to thrive.

One great part of self-compassion is we can decide how much of it we need in a given moment. We can be hard on ourselves when we feel it is needed or be gentle to ourselves when that is what's needed. Self-compassionate people recognize their suffering and respond with care and understanding rather than criticism and blame. They treat themselves with the same kindness as they would show to a good friend.

Benefits

The benefits of self-compassion are manifold: it's good for your physical health, your psychological health, and society. Physical health. Self-compassionate people are also happier and more resilient, and therefore they tend to be healthier physically. They use their social network better, so they're more apt to seek help when needed. Self-compassion is good for your immune system, your inflammatory system, and your autonomic nervous system because it decreases stress hormones and increases soothing ones.

Self-compassionate people tend to recover much more quickly from illness and medical procedures. They are also at lower risk for many mental and physical illnesses, including addiction, anxiety, depression, obesity, diabetes, heart disease, and chronic pain. In short—self-compassion is good medicine.

How to Practice Self-Compassion

Step 1: Notice the personal suffering

Notice the emotional pain you are going through (or have been through) and how it's affecting your physical body. Notice how it makes you feel to be suffering. And notice that this is normal, that this is what most people go through at some point in their lives.

Step 2: Mindfulness

Allow yourself to feel whatever it is you're feeling—emotions, aches and pains, anger, sadness (in short) without judgment or resistance. Simply notice them as they arise and pass.

Step 3: Kindness

Be kind to yourself. Accept that you are suffering. Talk to yourself as you would a close friend in the same situation, with warmth and support. At this point in the process, you may feel a sense of anger, judgment, or shame at yourself. This is completely natural and okay. Just note your feelings as they arise (anger, judgment, shame) and be gentle with them. Kindly say to yourself, "I am angry that I am angry because I am suffering." "I am tired of hurting because I am suffering." "I don't like how this is making me feel because I'm suffering." "I don't deserve to feel this way because I'm suffering." "This is not helpful; please help me get out of this state.

Step 4: Purpose

Have a purpose for your suffering. Notice what the purpose is and that it is a reason to be glad. It is a gift that allows you to grow, transform, let go of old patterns or habits, and become more mindful, open-hearted, and empathic. It can deepen your sense of connection with others and the world around you. And it can lead to gratitude for your life and for all of your experiences in general (including the trials).

Step 5: Commitment

Commit to living with intention. Be present with what you're feeling and do the best you can to work with it. Practice remembering a loving presence in your life and something good to be found within the experience. Try not to label or judge the experience, but simply observe it.

Why We Need to Practice Self-Compassion

Self-compassion allows us to become more resilient and freer in our lives. It allows us to be "good enough" for ourselves. It can protect us from depressions and anxiety. It can bring many people back into balance when they are suffering.

Practice self-compassion regularly, and you will cultivate the strength to stay balanced in your life, regardless of the ups or downs you experience on your journey. Self-compassion is not about being weak or being a pushover, and it's about being real.

We all want to be loved and accepted by others, but we also need to have compassion for ourselves. It's only then that we can truly excel in our lives—both professionally and personally. Also, self-compassion can strengthen your relationships with others because you will be more available to them and better forgive them when they let you down or make mistakes.

Method 13: *Remember What Makes You Happy*

If you've asked yourself how to become a happier person, this is already a very good sign. Awareness of your well-being is the first step to becoming a happier person. At a time when the world seems uncertain, we all need more joy in our lives.

It sounds like a cliché, but it's as true today as ever: well-being starts with your thoughts. Create inner peace by focusing on the positive aspects of your life and what makes you happiest. Stop dwelling on negative things and get rid of anything that doesn't make you happy. Whatever it is – the color of your walls, old memories that hurt to think about – let go of it! You can be happier without any sacrifice at all. It will take some time and patience to find out what makes you happy and replace anything that stands in the way.

When you become aware of what makes you happy, you can stop doing whatever it is that makes you unhappy.

1. Create a moment of peace. Whenever you start to feel overwhelmed, stop whatever you're doing and breathe deeply for a few moments. This will calm your nervous system and allow you to regain your focus and find happiness in the present moment instead of dwelling on the past or worrying about the future.

2. Get a sense of meaning and purpose in your life. Have a plan. If you're feeling down, or in despair, or don't have any goals and don't know what to do with your life, it is very easy to lose hope and feel like everything around you is meaningless. If you can't find a way, how are you going to survive when things get worse? You will need the ability to find happiness even if everything goes wrong. To find joy and purpose in your life when things worsen, first, cultivate happiness and a sense of purpose right now; start looking for ways to give meaning and purpose right now.

3. Find happiness in the small things. Don't compare yourself to others. Find contentment in the small things. This is the most important lesson you must learn: We don't live by comparison, and we should focus on what makes us happy, not what other people have or don't have. Your life can be filled with plenty of things if you stop obsessing over them. If a person raises their hand in class, just get up and walk away as quickly as possible. Don't waste your energy being bothered by stupid things that don't matter to you anyway. Focus on what does matter to you right now, stop obsessing about everything else we cannot change anyway; this will help give meaning to your life.

4. Be motivated by the pursuit of something bigger than yourself, even as it causes pain and suffering on the way to fulfillment. Achieving your goals is meaningless if you don't have the strength to pursue them. It's easy to be motivated by the pursuit of money, but wealth in itself is not enough. What's important in life is how we live, not just the things we acquire; a goal that everyone can achieve in their lifetime may be unimportant because it does not make us value our lives as much as something more meaningful and unique touches our hearts. If you want lasting happiness and fulfillment, work on becoming your best self and chasing after your goals with all your heart; achieve great things that no one else did before.

5. Cultivate virtues such as integrity, respect, patience, generosity, charity, and love for others – no matter what they do or say – as well as inner peace, which can be found by meditating on whatever leads you to feel at one with your spiritual nature (e.g., "Let go" or "Know Thyself"). To be happy, you must first have peace of mind and a sense of inner safety. If you don't have inner peace, your external situation won't matter. Your priorities must change; you must learn to be the master of your own life and to take control over what makes you happy today. You can only decide upon what makes you happy if you remember what made you happy in the past; this will give meaning to your life and open up your heart for more joy and gratitude.

6. Find balance in all your endeavors. Make time for things that make you feel happy and content. Figure out what makes you happy and how to be happy with whatever you have. The definition of joy is the same for everyone: finding something that gives you a sense of meaning and purpose. Happiness is feeling more contented with your current situation than your former situation would if you had been happier back then. If you find something that confuses you about what makes you happy, try to figure it out by thinking about what made you happier in the past and why; if you can't think of anything at all, then it probably doesn't make you happy.

7. Live in the moment and experience the moment for what it is, not a future or past. To be happy, you must endure pain and suffering, but you can't let it rule over you. You must stop worrying about the past or future. Ignorance is a curse; only knowledge will set you free from the bondage of happiness. When you learn how to be happy in your present life, then only will you have the strength to endure pain and suffering in the future. There is no point worrying about something that is beyond your control; worry is useless and meaningless. You can never take back what you have lost, nor can you undo any mistakes that have been made in the past.

To be happy, you must first learn to accept your present situation for what it is, not what you imagined it would be. You must find contentment in any situation that you are in. You can only accept and find happiness in certain situations if you stop blaming the world for making you unhappy; instead, try to change your perspective on life and turn nothing into something.

After finding peace through acceptance, the next step is accepting yourself: forgive yourself for past mistakes, soothe your soul with kindness and care because it is a waste of time to hate yourself for anything in the past.

Method 14:
Learn to Say "no"

Well, you are not alone. No is something many of my clients struggle with. When I ask them to say no, they respond with a resounding yes. I get it- being assertive feels uncomfortable when you've been putting your own needs last for so long.

Are you overcommitted? Do you have a hard time saying no when asked to take on more than what you can handle? Well, it's time for that to stop.

Some helpful pointers:

- Understand why it's so difficult to say no

- Learn some strategies for how to get out of an uncomfortable situation

- Recognize the signs that your yes is exceeding your capacity and make some changes!

Why it's So Difficult to Say no?

The most common causes of difficulty saying "no," are:

Fear: real or imagined. It can be fear of disappointing others or being judged, fear of coming across as unkind, rude or selfish, Fear of losing love or respect and being left out on a limb.

Guilt: guilt is what a person feels when they refuse to say no out of guilt. This is a mistake. It's the manager's job to ensure that employees can say no if they need to without shame and guilt. For example, if your boss asks you to take on a task that isn't in the job description, but you are experienced and decide it is something you want to do even though it's outside your duties and responsibilities. You can say no. Refusing to take on the task out of guilt is not an option. You have to.

Desire to keep a good relationship: This includes making excuses to other people or saying yes when you don't want to so that you can stay friends with the person asking for something that is not a job requirement.

Fear of failure: You've been telling yourself that you can't do it, but then you chicken out and say yes. Frequently, employees will say no to avoid the embarrassment of failing.

Fear of consequence: You know that sometimes saying no gets people angry or upset with you, so you don't want to risk this.

Shame: Short-changing yourself by making yourself feel bad about being asked for help when you know you can do it but are apprehensive and need extra support when saying no becomes difficult. Shaming yourself in front of others will only make matters worse by making others feel that you are identifying their needs higher than your own...which is exactly what you are doing.

Fear of repercussions: There might be repercussions if you say no. For instance, the person might feel angry or disappointed and shun you, or other family members don't want to see your face at any more family gatherings. The fear that they will not like you anymore is a real fear that can stop many from saying no when they need to consistently.

Avoid Burnout and Start Saying No. Here's How.

One of the most important skills a person can have is the ability to say "no". If you're overcommitted, you can be sure that your "yes" doesn't always reflect what you truly want. It can lead to burnout, which leads to resentment, and this is not what anyone wants. I have many clients come in and tell me they feel resentful of everyone who has a yes when struggling with a big fat NO.

As a therapist, I used to ask my clients if they wanted me to help them get out of the situation or wanted more information about how to handle it differently (this is an example of techniques for grounding yourself). They wanted more information, which is an example of how to say no. They were angry at the situation but didn't know how to frame it differently.

So what do you do if you want a bigger, fresher yes? Once again, it's all about saying no more often and better. We've all been in a situation where we feel like we can't say no and have to bite the bullet. Whether you are: an employee or a manager, it is time to stop saying yes when you don't want to. Many of us are so worried about getting things wrong that when someone asks us for help with something that doesn't belong at work, we say yes because we don't want to get into trouble.

Initially, this can feel very uncomfortable, but the result is an overall better experience of saying no, having more peace with it, and staying in the game longer.

This is how to stop saying yes when you mean no:

1. Recognize the warning signs of burnout and the telltale symptoms of saying "yes" when you want to say "no."
2. Developmental health strategies to handle any potential situation where you cannot say no, or stay away from the

situation that requires a lot of your time (family gatherings, travel plans, etc.).

3. Learn to reframe your thinking around saying "yes" without guilt or shame.

4. Learn how practicing saying no more often can bring you joy and freedom from feeling trapped and overly committed.

5. Practice with small tasks or situations that allow you to be flexible with your time and energy.

6. Be consistent. It is impossible to change a habit if you are not consistent about doing it (you'll slip up every other time!).

7. Ask for help if you need it, but remember that it is better to ask for help from someone who can give you an honest opinion or question because they are likely much more invested in you than the person who usually comes to mind when someone asks for your assistance.

8. Praise yourself for your saying no!

9. Watch yourself say no. You will likely find it challenging at first and need to practice. Keep at it! You'll feel the benefits of saying no in your soul very soon after you start practicing.

Here are some examples of how to say no:

"I am so glad you asked me about this, but my plate is full right now. I am not sure if I can fit that into my schedule, but I can check with Joe because he might be able to manage that project for you."

"Wow, thanks for offering to help Diana with that. I appreciate it, but I think she may have some other plans that may work out better for her. Let me ask her, and I'll let you know what I find out!"

"I am so sorry if that inconvenienced you. It wasn't my intention to cause a problem. To be honest, this is something that is causing me a lot of anxiety right now at work, and I have been working through some of the challenges to make sure it doesn't happen again."

It depends on the situation and what you can come up with that is true for you, so it is so important to practice this to know what to say, without feeling guilty or shame about it.

"We cannot always control our thoughts, but we can control how we act on them. As long as I act with integrity and take responsibility for my actions, I will be okay in the end.

Saying No Guilt-free

To say no, you must take responsibility for your words and actions. It is not a matter of blaming or judging the person asking; it is a matter of taking responsibility for what you are feeling. There is no shame in being honest, and there will always be something better in the future if you can say yes to someone else's request. Remember that saying no will help you create balance and space in your life because it will allow you to remember that things do not have to happen all at once.

Telling others about any issues or struggles can help work through them and develop solutions moving forward. This can be done with a family member, friend, or advisor.

It can also help to use the resources or people that are close to you. For instance, if you are having difficulty at work, talk to someone who knows what is going on and advise. If you are having trouble with schoolwork, talking to your professor may be helpful. Many people have been through similar situations and know how to handle them better than we students do.

The last thing I would like to mention is that everyone struggles at some point in time or another with being an adult. By taking responsibility for your actions, people will respect you more and also be able to trust that you will follow through on commitments that are made.

These steps will help you become more comfortable with saying no when necessary and when you need to make a healthy choice. This does not have to be an easy road, but it will be worth it in the end because there is a good chance everyone else involved with the situation will also benefit from your decision. You deserve to take care of yourself to focus on what is important and necessary, so do not worry about anything else at this point.

Every day, people are faced with the decision to say yes to one more task, one more obligation. But this growing sense of entitlement can lead to an overwhelming feeling of inadequacy and guilt, not just in our personal lives but also at work and in our relationships.

This vicious cycle eventually leads to an inability to say no, and people feel compelled to overcommit, underperform and avoid saying "I can't."

Say no to unrealistic deadlines and requests. When too many things are expected of us, we compromise our ability to complete tasks or deliver quality results.

Say no to more work than your job description requires. Going above and beyond in your job might be admirable, but doing so can detract from the time you need to take care of yourself or spend with friends and family.

Say no to tasks that negatively impact your happiness. Some tasks are stressful or even depressing, such as those that require you to fire employees or lay off loyal customers when business is slow. Saying "I can't" in these situations isn't career suicide – it's an act of self-preservation.

Say no when you have nothing left to give.

Method 15:
Learn to Delegate

Every day we are faced with tasks we want to do. So the next time you feel like delegating, read this chapter and get started! If you find yourself getting overloaded with work, or if it feels like your business is getting off track because you don't have enough time to take care of everything on your plate, it might be time for some delegation. There are two types: external and internal. For external delegation, you need an outside person or company to help complete the task. Internal delegation means handing off a task from one department to another here at the company.

There are many benefits to doing so. First and foremost is the time you gain by relieving yourself of the burden of completing a task. If you're not sure what to delegate off of, take a look below at some tips for getting started delegating.

One phrase that sums up delegation is "if it ain't broke, don't fix it." That means if the current system works in your business, there is no need to change it. Trust that it will go smoothly, and don't be afraid to delegate a task.

What is Delegation?

Delegation is a role in which one person gives another person control and responsibility for part of his or her work. It's also a strategy where an employee asks another employee to take on a job.

Delegation in the Workplace

Many managers view delegation as a way to get more done with fewer people. It's also a popular way to handle noncritical tasks that aren't top priorities. However, delegation isn't just about assigning busy work or giving employees more responsibilities because you have too much work on your plate.

Delegation Tips

Here are some tips to help you get started delegating and get the most out of your employees:

Put yourself in your employees' shoes. How would you feel if someone were asking you to do something? Imagine yourself being criticized by your boss or co-workers if you could not complete a task on time. Delegate tasks before they cause problems so that there are no consequences later.

Decide what's most important for each task. If you're going to be late because of a miscommunication, choose another task to delegate first. Also, remember that change is always difficult and often uncomfortable at first. If you find that your employees are taking too much time to complete their tasks, try to come up with a plan so they can do it quickly.

If you're going to be late because of a miscommunication, choose another task to delegate. Remember the goal of delegation. While one person is assigned the "heavy" load, every employee has a purpose in life and should be proud of his or her work.

Delegating Effectively

Delegating is a valuable skill that will help you and your business grow. Throughout your career, you may find yourself spending more time delegating than doing the work yourself. This could be a challenge for those who struggle with delegating in the workplace. Here are some tips for being able to delegate effectively.

Understand what you want to accomplish: if you do not know what task you want to delegate, don't! As an entrepreneur, this is often easier said than done but try to start small and go there. Determine where and how you can delegate or assign certain tasks without compromising the bigger picture of your goals for your business or organization.

Know your strengths and weaknesses: while you may be an expert in certain business areas, delegate the areas that you know are not a strong suit for you to focus on what you excel at. It would help if you also considered delegating tasks that may not be your first choice of work but are necessary, nonetheless. For example, if you have trouble keeping up with paperwork or filing, delegate this task to someone else.

Technology is a wonderful tool to aid in your delegation of tasks. Countless apps will help you get out of danger when it comes to your social media posts, and there are even apps that connect you with individuals who can help you with specific tasks. For example, if you need help with ongoing blog posts, find someone who will do it for just the cost of their expenses. On LinkedIn, I have connected myself with individuals who can edit my work and make suggestions to improve my writing skills or content creation in general.

Be a good delegator: while you may have to delegate tasks yourself, remember to be open and honest with your employees to know their goals and the expectations for how they need to work with you.

When delegating, make sure that you are fair to everyone involved. There is no embarrassment in knowing that it is not your fault if something goes wrong because someone else made a mistake or could not follow through on their part of the agreement.

Doing and Delegating

The first step is deciding the scope of the task, "does it make good business sense?" If any part of the process is getting in your way, you may want to consider a different person to work on that part or alter the process. If there isn't a clear delineation to what needs to be done and who will do it, then delegate it to someone in your department. 'What's your role?' is a great question to ask yourself when delegating.

If you want someone else to do something for you, ask them if they are willing and able. Don't just assume they can or will do it. Here are some tips on getting started. Delegate a task on the pipeline from your timesheet, list all of the tasks you need to complete by the end of the day. Look at past pipeline reports and determine how long it usually takes a certain item to get through. Now figure out how many people are working on that task (what's your staff capacity) and use that as a guide for assigning that task.

Start with simple assignments, like rearranging photos or making notes in a spreadsheet template. Don't overwhelm them with too much at once, so they don't become discouraged and lose interest.

Here are some ideas:

1. Take the high road and delegate more. Delegate some tasks away from yourself so that you can focus on bigger things.

2. Get an outside perspective or external help to ensure that you're not unreasonable when it comes to delegating tasks.

3. Learn how to say no and recognize when you need a bit of time off to take care of your personal life – including dealing with your stress at work – so that you will be able to do both wells in the end! Remember, delegation takes time, and if you're delegating just the right tasks to people in your business, you'll be able to spend the time on the things that matter most.

How to Delegate Effectively

1) Start small with simple tasks. Give yourself time to learn the ins and outs of delegation before stepping up to larger projects.

2) Don't try to be a perfectionist in delegating. An overwhelming amount of work can cause a breakdown in your project, so make sure you know what you're getting into before you start.

3) Know when it's time to change delegators. If the project is not going the way, it should reassess your delegation strategy and see if there is another way that works better for everyone involved. The more you do this, the better you will determine when changes need to be made or when someone else should be given more responsibility.

4) Be clear about the quality of work you expect. If you don't clearly define what is expected of the person, they will not know how to meet your standard, causing confusion and frustration on both sides.

5) Give feedback on how they can improve while giving them a chance to work through their mistakes. When delegating, it is important to be open and honest so that everyone knows where they stand.

6) Set goals for yourself and the person that you are delegating to. This will help provide structure for both you and your employee or contractor.

7) Delegate to competent and skilled people, not necessarily popular or the most senior person on your team.

Getting in the Right Mindset

The important thing to remember is patience. Setting goals is good, but not at the cost of micromanaging your employees. When delegating to a new employee, make sure to set goals that are reasonable and attainable. Start small and build on what you have learned from the start. The keyword here is "build". Don't give up when you don't get immediate results. You may be losing them for the long term if you do. Let them do their jobs and find themselves far less stressed and more productive and provide a better work environment for your employees.

Importance of being a delegate

As a leader, it is important to understand the importance of delegation skills. Delegation is a skill that you develop and hone throughout your career. If you are having difficulty with delegation, ask for help from a colleague or mentor who may know some effective strategies to help you.

Being successful as an entrepreneur - and one of the most successful entrepreneurs - means being good at all the different aspects of running a business. This includes running day-to-day operations while still having enough time to focus on long-term growth and planning for your future success.

When delegating tasks, make sure you delegate something tangible that can be accomplished in a specific amount of time with specific results in mind. If you are delegating a project that you know may take much more time than expected, make sure to keep yourself accountable by setting a specific date when you expect to see the results.

Delegating effectively, especially in a small business setting, requires understanding and using each person's strengths. You should delegate tasks based on the competency of each individual rather than based on seniority or their popularity among staff. Consider creating a formal process for people to follow to ensure that all tasks are completed correctly and with minimal frustration on both sides.

Once you have delegated work out, be sure to create accountability and next action plans that will help keep everyone moving forward until they are finished with their project.

Why Delegate?

First and foremost, delegation frees up time. If you're overloaded with deadlines, meetings, and other tasks, this is a great way to free up some of that time. It can allow you more work-life balance since delegating will ensure your work gets done while you're away from the office. It also helps improve your team's morale by giving them a chance to develop new skills and learn how to be leaders in their own right.

To get started delegating:

1. Focus on what you want to get done – Define goals and tasks as specifically as you can so you can give the task to someone else. Writing down your goals will ensure that you don't delegate something important or miss-communicate about what is being delegated. This will also help you determine whether or not the task has been completed by someone else to know if it should be given back or something that may need to be done.

2. Avoid micromanagement - If you think you will monitor and take care of every task delegated, it probably isn't worth delegating. If you don't want to appear like a micromanager and ensure the desired results are being met, you mustn't micro-manage the person or team doing the work.

3. Be honest – If this will be a temporary or a long-term solution, let your employee know so they can plan accordingly. Also, if there are any special considerations you need to make based on your company culture or industry, let everyone know as well. This will help the person or team you delegate off so that they aren't caught off guard. Some jobs may require a lot of brainpower, for example, and the employee may not focus completely due to other things on their mind. Delegation is a great way to get more time while still working with the people you want to work with. The situation and person must be right, though, to work out effectively for this type of working relationship.

4. Avoid comparisons – This is one of the biggest mistakes individuals can make when delegating a task. When delegating, you mustn't compare the work or time spent on the project to someone else's. Let the person you are delegating off do their best job and make sure that they have all of the resources and ability to complete a good job.

5. Don't be afraid of failure – Not everyone will always get something right on their first try. That is why it is important not to expect perfection but rather focus on improvement. If your company culture works well with accountability, then hold this person accountable for their results.

Method 16:
Get Enough Sleep

How much sleep do you need? If you've ever been plagued with sleep burnout, you know how bad it can be. You might feel tired all the time, forgetful, irritable, and apathetic. And while it may seem like something that's just a part of life to tolerate if you want to get anything done in your day-to-day work and personal life, research has debunked that notion.

Recent research has shown that the average adult needs 7 to 8 hours of sleep for optimal memory function. That's about an hour longer than many people report getting regularly. But a lack of sleep doesn't just affect your ability to function normally. It can also impact your mental health, which can be a serious matter for your overall well-being. For example, while some sleep-deprived people appear to function just fine when they're not getting enough rest, others might be more prone to mood swings or anxiety.

Robust evidence shows a positive link between sleep deprivation and the development of psychological problems such as depression and anxiety. And what's perhaps more concerning is that this connection is independent of whether you get less sleep than others in general.

How Sleep Helps Burnout?

There are some pretty compelling reasons why sleep is so important. While it's dubbed the "sleep hormone" or the "happiness hormone," research has shown that people who don't get enough sleep can be more irritable than those who do.

In addition, we know that memory and learning are very dependent on sleep. Without the right amount of sleep, you can expect to have memory lapses in your day-to-day life. Sleep is also linked to a lower risk for illnesses such as colds and even pneumonia.

This was one of the conclusions from a recent study, which showed that people without enough sleep were 12 times more likely to develop acute respiratory illnesses like pneumonia than well-rested people. Because sleep helps regulate your immune system, it's essential if you want to keep those health risks at bay.

If you have trouble sleeping or don't get enough shut-eye, it can also exacerbate feelings of anxiety and depression. If our brains run on deep sleep cycles in which slow-wave brain waves are dominant, they can retain and use new information more effectively during our waking hours. All of this helps explain why a good night's sleep can make you happier and more focused. And that's important if you find yourself starting to feel the burnout effect.

Mild sleep deprivation or sleep debt can make it tough for you to feel upbeat, positive, and productive. But when your fatigue becomes extended over time, it can have some pretty serious consequences on your mind and body.

You might wonder then, how much sleep do I need? If you're not getting enough, it can start to impact your health.

Recent research has shown that a lack of sleep is linked to:

1. A weakened immune system leaves you more vulnerable to illness and infection.

2. A weakened heart muscle makes it harder for your body to pump blood effectively.

3. Increased risk of obesity and diabetes because lack of sleep makes it harder for your body to process glucose (sugar).

4. Mood swings can lead to irritability, anxiety, and depression.

5. Slower reaction times and a reduced attention span could raise the risk of accidents at work or home.

6. Higher risk of premature death, according to the National Institutes of Health.

So how can you get enough sleep? While some people do fine on less sleep, the only way to know if you're getting enough is to track it.

One way to measure how much sleep you need is by tracking your patterns of normal sleeping times and wake-up times over several days or a week. Several apps can help you keep a record of when you went to bed and when you woke up so that you can figure out your optimal sleep schedule. This must be done consistently over time because it gives your body a chance to establish its normal patterns.

Having Trouble Sleeping?

If you're not getting to the recommended amount of sleep, it's okay. It doesn't mean that you need to go on a crash diet or get rid of your pets.

Thus, you need to be more conscious about the amount of sleep you're getting and set realistic limits about how much sleep your body can handle at any given time.

Don't set unrealistic goals for yourself. Some people try to get 8 hours of sleep every night and find that they can't consistently get it, which leads to feelings of frustration and impatience.

A better strategy is to establish realistic goals. Get a good night's sleep every night for a week or two. After that, if you still don't feel rested, then put an alarm on your phone so you can wake up as soon as you hit the point of being comfortably sleepy. That will help you determine how much sleep your body needs at any given time.

More than anything, just be sure that you don't try to force yourself into getting enough sleep when it might not be possible for your body.

Insomnia

Insomnia is a term used to describe your inability to fall asleep or stay asleep. It's more than just being tired or having trouble falling asleep. That said, you can get insomnia even if you feel rested, but it might be a symptom of another condition that you should be aware of.

For example, you might have sleep apnea if you're snoring loudly and can't breathe during the night despite feeling rested. You might also have insomnia if you find that it takes something like an hour for your body to settle down enough so that you can fall asleep.

No matter the cause of your insomnia, you might feel restless and unsatisfied when you wake up, which can lead to some serious issues.

It can make it difficult for you to feel alert throughout the day, and it can also make it hard to get through the workday at a consistent pace.

Some people even report feeling depressed or not wanting to go out in public when they haven't gotten enough sleep.

All in all, insomnia has been linked to short and long-term health effects like:

1. Increased stress levels can lead to higher blood pressure.
2. Increased risk of depression because having insomnia makes it harder for you to stay focused throughout the day.
3. Increased risk of heart disease because insomnia has been linked to an increased risk of death from heart attacks and strokes.
4. Increased risk of obesity because sleep-deprived people are more likely to overeat and give in to emotional eating.
5. Increased risk of diabetes because lack of sleep makes it harder for your body to process glucose (sugar).
6. Slower reaction times and a reduced attention span could raise the risk of accidents at work or home.
7. Higher chance of premature death, according to the National Institutes of Health.
8. Chronic pain because sleep-deprived people have more pain and are more susceptible to injury.

And the list goes on.

Suffering from insomnia can mess with your life, so it's important to figure out what's causing your insomnia so that you can figure out a way to deal with it. It's not just about getting to bed at a good time but also about figuring out how you manage to get enough sleep when you don't feel like you want or need it.

One of the most common reasons for insomnia is stress.

How to Improve Sleep Hygiene

I'm always amazed by how many people say they don't have trouble getting to sleep or waking up early. The truth is that it doesn't take much to improve your sleep hygiene so that you can get enough quality sleep every night.

First, set realistic limits about how long you can stay awake at night and when you want to wake up. It may sound silly, but the only way to know if you can get enough sleep at night is by putting a plan in place for yourself and sticking with it for a few weeks.

If your partner wakes up before you do, don't worry about it. Turn off the alarm and try to get as much sleep as you can in chunks so that you can wake up early naturally rather than forcing yourself to do it with an alarm. This will help your body remember when it needs to wake up so you can get more consistent results over time.

Many people trying to change their sleep schedule have a tough time sleeping because they love to go to bed late. It's better for your health if you go to bed earlier, but don't be concerned if it takes some time for you to change your habits.

If you go out at night, try not to spend too long on your phone or tablet screen before hitting the hay. The blue light from your screen can mess with the natural hormones in your body that give you a sense of relaxation.

If you have trouble getting to sleep, consider putting on a pair of socks as soon as you get into bed. The dark color and constriction around your feet are like nature's own sleeping aid and can help you feel drowsy so that you can fall asleep faster.

If your anxiety revs up every night, try doing some deep breathing exercises every day so that it's easier for you to relax at night. You could also buy some lavender essential oil and put a few drops in the air before going to bed every night.

"You are what you think you are," so you must think of yourself as someone who can get enough sleep every night and set limits about how long you should stay awake at night. Ask yourself if getting enough sleep is the most important thing in life or if there's something else that you wish could take priority. It doesn't matter what sleeping habits you develop, but it does matter how much sleep your body needs at any given time.

Don't get overwhelmed with thinking about how many hours of sleep you need every day. Instead, prioritize your quality of sleep by getting the right amount of rest. You can start with a good bedtime routine and see if you can set limits for yourself. If you have trouble falling asleep, it's okay to put an alarm on your phone so that you know when to wake up.

Remember that sleep is very important for your mental and physical health, so it's best to find a way to get enough sleep each night at the right time.

Method 17:
Eat Well

As the days lengthen and the temperature continues to rise, it's important to take care of your health to maintain wellness. Eating well enables you to get the most out of your workout sessions while also giving you a sense that all is good in life.

Burnout is no joke, and with overuse comes pain. Taking care of yourself helps to prevent injury; doing so also makes you better at your job.

Essential to Eat Well

The best way to maintain a healthy diet is to prepare your food yourself. I know that buying pre-packaged meals like frozen pizza or instant noodles may save you time, but they are usually high in sodium, low in nutrition, and taste terrible! Not only will eating home-cooked meals help your body better absorb nutrients, but energy levels will also be steadier without the blood sugar spikes and crashes from processed foods.

How much should you eat?

1) Highly active people with a good appetite should aim for 1.5-2g of protein for every kg of body weight. For example, if you weigh 70kg (155pounds), aim for at least 105-140g of protein per day.

2) For most adults, 1.4g-1.8g of protein per kg of body weight.

3) The Institute of Medicine recommends 1.6g-2.0g for adults, but this is based on a 2000 calorie diet.

4) Vegetarians should aim to eat 7-10 servings of vegetables and fruit per day, in addition to the protein requirement outlined above.

5) See the USDA resources below for recommended daily consumption amounts.

Is There a Stress Management Diet?

If you are experiencing an increased level of stress and tension in your life, then a diet can help. In this case, eating well for burnout is not enough. There need to be other ways to manage stress and control your health. A good example of a part of the lifestyle that will encourage healthy habits is relaxation exercises.

Choosing between a hobby or a self-improvement project can be very helpful because it rewards you with pleasure when you achieve results, instead of the reward being some new electronic gadget.

Practicing relaxation exercises outside of work hours will help release endorphins, making us feel good about ourselves and content with our lives.

One way to start is by holding five minutes at the beginning and end of each day. Muscle relaxation can be encouraged by lying on your back and breathing deeply, starting at the toes and moving up to your head. This helps to activate the parasympathetic nervous system, which is calming.

Again, small steps with regular practice help develop good habits that last throughout life. Eating well for burnout is a part of this process, and learning to relax to stay healthy over time.

The amount of stress you feel will determine how much exercise you should have per week. Again, there is an inverse relationship between exercise and stress levels. A healthy diet can improve your mood, reduce anxiety and prevent depression. Eating well is essential to stress management since it's impossible to feel happy or refreshed with an empty stomach. Stress is also known to weaken the immune system -- leading to cold and flu season right around exam time.

You must find ways to relieve stress since prolonged stress can lead to high blood pressure, heart disease, and digestive problems. It can even affect your memory! Unfortunately, there's no one size fits all approach for stress management, and what works for one person may not work for another.

Foods for Stress Relief

It's easy to get overwhelmed that we face these days, especially at work. Eating well for stress is important because it helps keep you healthy and energized while giving you the energy to deal with your problems. A diet high in carbohydrates and low in fiber can increase blood sugar and cause fatigue. In contrast, a diet high in fat and low in protein can lead to anxiety or depression due to nutritional deficiencies.

The best way to battle stress is by eating high iron foods (and thus have other positive effects). Foods such as lean meat, green vegetables, and dark green leafy vegetables offer significant quantities of iron.

Iron is essential for our nervous system, and while both men and women should aim for 8mg of iron per day, women are more prone to developing anemia and feeling the effects of stress. Women menstruating should eat 16mg per day.

Foods that are rich in Vitamin C also help with stress relief. They boost the immune system and prevent disease, which helps protect against severe stress. The best sources of Vitamin C include citrus fruits such as oranges and tangerines, guava, and kiwi.

Foods high in calcium, such as milk, yogurt, or cheese, may help you feel less stressed because it helps manage your emotions. Caffeine can help you maintain your energy levels for hours, but too much may make your heart race and disturb your sleep. Avoid or moderate your caffeine intake if you experience anxiety or jitters as a result of drinking coffee.

Foods high in Vitamin B6 may help you feel less stressed as well. They are found in bananas, avocados, fish, and red meat. If you eat foods with higher amounts of B6 but are still feeling stressed, try supplementing 10mg per day to keep your emotions in check. Some people may be more susceptible to stress due to poor diets high in simple carbohydrates or processed foods.

People under extreme stress may find it difficult to concentrate or think clearly. To prevent clumsiness, dizziness, and headaches, make sure to eat foods rich in iron, calcium, and vitamins B1 and B6. The best sources of these nutrients are lean meat, green vegetables, and dark green leafy vegetables.

Foods high in Vitamin A such as carrots, cantaloupe, or broccoli may help protect your eyes from the effects of stress. Best food sources of vitamin A include carrots, cantaloupe, broccoli, and leafy greens such as spinach or Swiss chard.

Foods high in Vitamin E may help manage stress because it reduces inflammation in the body caused by oxidative stress on your cells. The best sources of Vitamin E are almonds, sunflower seeds, and olives.

Foods high in calcium may help you feel less stressed because it helps to manage your emotions. Caffeine can help you maintain your energy levels for hours, but too much may make your heart race and disturb your sleep. Avoid or moderate caffeine intake if you experience anxiety or jitters as a result of drinking coffee.

Foods high in magnesium may help manage stress because it is needed for relaxing muscles and relaxing the nervous system.

Your body is the essential tool you have, so it makes sense that you want to do everything you can to take care of it. It is easy to eat unhealthy food when available or when eating out, but making an effort to eat well and eat healthily can help you achieve optimal health.

Always remember that what goes in your mouth comes out through your bottom! If a food is not nutritionally sound, then it will have negative effects on your body. If you want to be healthier and feel better about yourself, then remember that prevention is worth a pound of cure with an ounce of prevention! So make eating awesome!

Method 18:
Take Time for Yourself - Guilt-free

We're all busy. We have commitments, obligations, and a plethora of responsibilities to juggle. Making time for ourselves isn't always easy. But it's worthwhile. The key is to find your way of doing it--what makes sense for you. We have five ways that you can take time for yourself guilt-free.

2. Let go of perfectionism
3. Do something that nurtures your body
4. Do something that nurtures your mind
5. Set boundaries with others
6. Spend quality time with yourself

Some people find it's helpful to schedule time for themselves, like planning a trip away to visit friends or going to their favorite restaurant every Sunday. Other people find it's helpful to have a window each day in their schedules when they can take a break and not feel guilty about doing something good for themselves. Some people even schedule their guilt-free time, writing it into their calendars.

You have to determine what works best for you and how you can regularly make time for yourself. That might mean setting specific times to do something fun or relaxing and not feeling bad if you don't make it happen every day, but doing your best to keep the commitment.

Guilt-Free Ways to Make Time for Yourself

We all have to make time for ourselves, but there is a stigma attached to doing something simply for your enjoyment and shortening the time we spend on "work." We do not feel like we are accomplishing anything by taking time for ourselves.

Taking time for yourself is important, especially in this fast-paced world where we are pushed too hard and too far. We can accomplish all of our tasks and still take time to enjoy the things that make us happy and bring us peace. Unfortunately, most people can achieve this by guilt-tripping themselves into it. If they do not feel guilty, they will not think about it often enough.

There are many ways that guilt-free time can be obtained, but we do not feel guilty about enjoying ourselves. There is a stigma, and we, like people, have to come to see it less as a burden and more as an opportunity.

Take time for yourself guilt-free by following these ideas:

1. Take Extended Time for Yourself -The most important thing to do is just commit to being around your house for a short time. This way, you will not be looking at your watch and constantly feel guilty. You will allow a small amount of time to come and go, but you will not feel frustrated that it is passing by so quickly only because you have taken the time to yourself. This can be from 10 minutes up to an hour and a half if you have the time. The important thing is that you are relaxed enough to focus on the activity at hand and not feel the need to rush back out into the world.

2. Take Daily Self-Care Time - This is something often overlooked but is important. Take a short break each day to do something to take care of yourself. This can be meditation, a walk, reading a book, or anything else that brings you peace and feels good. You don't have to do this each day if it doesn't appeal to you, but it will help lighten the load.

3. Make Time That Matter Most - Don't let the things that matter most to you slip through the cracks. There are so many distractions in our lives today. Even if we are not doing anything else, we are likely to be checking email or social media. You can make time for what is important to you by scheduling your time. Even if it is just 10 minutes a day, schedule it into your calendar as guilt-free time.

4. Take Time for You - If you are not taking the time for yourself, you are likely taking too much time from someone else.

5. Be Mindful - Accept the fact that you are busy. Remind yourself it is okay to have some time for yourself and be included in your weekly schedule. When you are finished with your guilt-free time, don't feel guilty about enjoying yourself. It is okay to take some break from the important things until you can come back and focus on them. We spend too much time in this fast-paced world and too little time enjoying what is important. Take a small amount of time to yourself every day and let the rest of the busy moments pass by without guilt or anxiety. Take a moment every day to be honest with yourself-how did I do today?

6. Don't Punish Yourself - There is no need to punish yourself! If you are taking time for yourself, it is likely because you deserve it. You work hard and have a lot of responsibilities, so don't be so hard on yourself! You cannot be perfect, and if you beat yourself up over not taking enough "me" time, it will only serve to make you feel worse about the whole thing and cause more stress.

7. Listen to Your Body - The most important thing to do when it comes to taking time for yourself is to listen to your own body. Your body needs some downtime, and if you feel guilty about taking time for yourself, perhaps this guilt can be avoided if you take the time for yourself.

8. Take an Abundance of Breaks - Abundance is very important, and taking breaks helps you feel relaxed a lot easier than if you are continually feeling stressed. Getting time for yourself every day and every week will help you be less stressed overall. Take a break throughout the day, and have several breaks within your busy week. If you can manage your time well, you can find time each day to experience peace and relaxation. Take some time to unplug from the world and get away from your responsibilities.

9. Take Time to Simplify - It is difficult to take time for yourself if you feel overwhelmed by everything you need to do. Simplifying your life is a great way to have some guilt-free time on the side. But if you want some tips, read out an article on some of the ways that an organized home and an organized lifestyle will help you feel better about yourself and your day.

10. Be Creative and Make Things - If you feel guilty about taking time for yourself, the best thing you can do is create something. You don't have to make anything spectacular. As long as you create something (even if you make a mess), it will take away some of your stress and guilt. Play around with different crafts to see what interests you. Create a scrapbook or collage so you can archive all of your memories. You could even write down your thoughts, journal, or just draw a picture.

11. Do Something That Makes You Happy - Your health and happiness are two things that are worth investing in. The best thing you can do is simply skip the guilt and get out and do something that makes you happy. If this is not something that appeals to you, then go somewhere else for a few hours. Spend time with a friend or family member. Do something you enjoy doing, not something you feel guilty about because you are skimping on your responsibilities or work. Take some time for yourself, and it will make you feel better if nothing else!

12. Be Helpful to Others - For many people, helping others can be a way to get the guilt of having some time for yourself out of your mind. There are always needs in just about every town and community. Someone needs food, someone needs a ride somewhere, or someone needs something fixed around the house. This can be a great way to make yourself feel better about the time that you have arranged in your day for yourself. Taking time for yourself by helping someone else can be easier to swallow if you don't look at it as a selfish act.

13. Take Time for Yourself in the Morning Before The Day Gets Started - If you want to take time for yourself first off, do it in the morning. This way, you don't have to worry about it as the day goes on, and you can feel guilt-free. Do something that makes you happy!

14. Make a Plan to Take Time For Yourself - If you want to take time for yourself a lot, you need to make it a priority. Planners are great for helping people remember what they have to do, so I highly recommend purchasing one of them! Try not to make things too ambitious at first. Start with doing something simple and small and build from there.

15. Be in Control of Your Schedule - If you want to take time for yourself, the last thing that you will need is to have your schedule dictated by other people. Make your rules and stick with them.

16. Learn to Enjoy Your Time by Yourself - Some people just don't like being with themselves. These people need to work on this issue a bit. If you don't enjoy your time by yourself, this might make it more difficult to take the time to do what you want and need to do or even want to do!

The key to finding guilt-free time for yourself is to make sure you do something that makes you feel good about yourself. You can take the time for yourself, guilt-free, and you will feel better for it--as long as what you are doing makes you feel accomplished or at least a little better about your life.

Taking the time to be thoughtful about how we want to live our lives is important. It's easy to catch up on other things and not think about what makes us happy or fulfilled. We can waste our time on things that do not matter and miss out on the things. Taking some guilt-free time for ourselves will help us avoid making this mistake.

It is important to take time, guilt-free, and you can do it if you try. Simply look at your day-to-day schedule and decide how you want to change it. Make small changes that are easy to make and stick with so you do not fall off the wagon when things get busy again.

Method 19:
Get Support from Loved Ones

Perhaps you have been experiencing a lot of stress lately, but you just don't know what to do about it. This chapter will provide some expert advice and information on burnout.

Burnout is not always associated with the work one does, but it is due to too much stress that people can't handle in many cases. We all have certain limits that we need to maintain, and when these limits are breached, we suffer from negative feelings such as depression or anxiety, which can be very hard to control.

If you work a full-time job and still have the main responsibility of taking care of your family, it would be a good idea to find more help. You may not even have realized how much stress you are under, as in most cases, people focus on helping others before giving themselves any help. It is important to make time for yourself, no matter how little it is.

Remember that no one can do everything by themselves, and we all need some kind of help at one point or another.

Seek family advice

Get close to those who care about you the most, and ask them what would be the best decision to make regarding your stress.

If the family can provide the right advice, it will be time well spent because understanding their perspective will better understand the problem. You may also have found out that they don't have all the answers, but at least you know that they understand what is going on in your life, and for this reason, they are great people to depend on.

Ask Friends for Help

If you feel that no one close to you can give you advice that will help, do not hesitate to look at other places. Friends are always great sources of information, even if they don't have the same levels of stress issues that you have. Having friends is a great way to let off some steam and talk about what is troubling you. It is very beneficial to your mental health. You may not need professional help, but rather a friendly ear with experience in this kind of thing.

Meditation

If you are used to taking some time out in a day, then meditating is a great way to help deal with issues. It would be best if you never overwhelm yourself by doing too much at once. You can work out, meditate, and get a good night's sleep in one day if needed though you should never feel pressured to do so. So taking some time out every day is very beneficial for your emotional well-being. Once you grasp things, you can start to do more things one day, but if you don't feel comfortable doing so, lower your expectations slightly.

Professional help

Not every problem has an answer or solution available to it, and some problems simply get too complex to solve on your own. You must seek professional help. A professional is specially trained to deal with such problems, and you can rest assured that they will take care of your problem with the highest level of professionalism. Do not ignore any problem and try your best to seek help as soon as you can.

You must take your time to handle stress in the best way possible. Maintaining a proper balance between work and family can be difficult, but it is not impossible.

Method 20:
Work Part-time

If you can afford it, ask your employer to reduce your work hours too, perhaps, just four days a week. This way, you'll be able to devote the other three days of the week to your personal life (taking care of errands, seeing family and friends) and pursue a hobby that brings you joy. The occasional break from work will help you stay fresh and creative while also boosting your self-confidence.

A great way to prevent burnout is by setting aside certain periods or days of the week for work only; this will help keep your work identity whole and not spread out over your whole life. You can also schedule other "work" times, such as sitting down and editing a report or proofreading a document. This way, you won't feel like you're "working" because you have to make small corrections on your work.

Lastly, try to take time off at least once a year. This will help maintain the freshness of your work by giving you a chance to recharge. If you don't take time off, your work identity can easily become an extension of yourself. By taking a break, you'll be able to more easily see where the line lies between "you" and "your job." And if you learn to see the two as separate entities, it will be easier to maintain a healthy work-life balance.

Working Part-time

If you can't work full-time and need to keep your income consistent on a part-time basis, knowing how to deal with burnout can be especially important.

I've compiled this list of tips for dealing with work burnout for those who work part-time jobs, both hoping that it will help those who are currently experiencing it and so that they may avoid it.

1) Recognize when you're feeling burnt out. Do you find yourself feeling sluggish or unmotivated? Or do you feel like the tasks at hand are taking longer than they should and aren't being completed quite as well as usual? These are some signs of overworked feelings and are a good indication that you need to take a few days off to get back on track and finish up the work so that you can get your full-time job done as well as possible.

2) Schedule some time off from the projects at hand and use that time to see what else is going on in your life. Normally, we feel like it's necessary to handle our responsibilities without even thinking about other aspects of our life when we work. You just have to check in with yourself and see how you're handling those other things because if something's not right, it probably won't be right when you're working on the jobs you feel pressured to do.

3) Take time to enjoy yourself. It's very easy to get caught up in the routine of a 9-5 job, but you have to remember that life goes on outside of work. Use some of your off time to do the things that make you happy, whether that's going out with friends or playing board games with your family. If you're having a tough day at work, it can be helpful to step away from the stress and relax in your free time before returning to work refreshed and ready for anything.

4) Schedule hobbies into your week with regularity. It's very easy only to do the things you're used to doing, but try to remember that you can

do anything for a few hours a week. Whether it's playing an instrument, working out, or going to a book club meeting, it can be good for your stress levels and brain health to spend some time challenging yourself in new ways.

5) Find support outside of work. Whether you have friends who are in the same boat as you are, our family members and spouses who understand your situation, reaching out for help when you need it will only help you face challenges with more effectiveness. Whether it's your boss, your co-workers, or even the people at work who are treating you well and showing a lot of support, it's important to stay in touch with people.

6) Encourage yourself. Ask for help when you need it, and don't be afraid to say "no" if the task is a job you're not good at doing. If you've been burnt out recently, taking recovery time is important and does require some effort. Don't feel like there's no point in trying if you've already failed once or twice before.

7) Take breaks from your computer during long periods of the day. During long periods where you're not planning much of anything, taking a break from your computer can be very helpful. I always find that I can get a lot more done if I take a break for at least half an hour on the weekends. Once your brain returns to the "listening to itself" mode, it's in when you're not doing anything and can make new ideas and connections, and it becomes easier to jump back into the deep end of any new project.

8) Don't let people push you into doing something as a result of pressure. This can be the hardest thing to deal with when you're in a position with a lot of responsibility, but it's important to remember that

you don't have to get everything done at once. Take time with the work instead of trying to rush through it and make mistakes.

9) Make sure you enjoy what you're doing. I know many people in situations where they don't enjoy what they do, which can be very stressful over the long term. Try to find something within your part-time job that motivates you, whether it's talking with certain people or testing out new techniques on each project.

10) Challenge yourself to learn new things every so often. If your work involves only a few things, making an effort to figure out new skills related to what you're working on can become very fulfilling. Try to find opportunities for this with your boss or co-workers, and you'll be able to experience something that can do the rest of the job more interesting.

11) Make sure you have a life outside of work. This is very important because it's easy to get caught up in a cycle where all you're doing is working and trying to work at the same time. Once you let yourself grow out of that mindset, it becomes easier to focus on what matters while still keeping your job responsibilities in check.

12) Find new ways of doing things every so often. Depending on where you get hired, the kind of company you work for, or even the nature of your part-time job, there's probably going to be routine and always the same. Find ways to mix things up as much as possible so that it doesn't get stale.

13) Challenge yourself to improve over time. If your job seems more of a dead-end, take charge and try to change things for yourself. You'll feel more fulfilled when trying to make something better out of what you already have instead of giving up and going in a completely different direction.

14) Count your blessings if you can keep things under control. It's very easy to get caught up in the little things that can drive you crazy at work, and it's also easy to feel like your life is out of control if you're unemployed for a long time. The world isn't going to turn into a nice place if you let yourself feel like that, so keep a strong head and remind yourself of the advantages of having stable employment.

15) Be realistic about what kind of job you can get. There are certain qualifications or special skills that can make it easier for someone to get a full-time position, but in most cases, there will be some form of obstacles between where you are now and where you want to be.

Be Productive

If you find that your work is taking up a lot of your time and preventing you from doing other things, perhaps it's time to reassess the kinds of tasks you're asking yourself to do. In the long run, if you constantly ask yourself to do unimportant tasks, these kinds of busy work are just wasted time.

The first step to finding more productive ways to spend your time is figuring out what tasks you should be doing. Take the time to think about everything that's happening around you, and try to determine which tasks are necessary and which are just a waste of time. Then, work on eliminating the unnecessary ones, or at least making sure the essential ones get done on time so that they don't become a distraction for you.

Stay Creative

If you find that you're constantly repeating the same tasks in your job, making minor changes here and there but nothing really "changing," perhaps it's time to start looking at other options. After all, if you hate your job, how can you find joy in doing your work? That may sound a bit extreme at first, but take a moment to think about it. The best way to stay creative is by stepping outside of yourself.

Method 21:
Change jobs

If you're feeling burnt out at work and don't know where to turn, we have the perfect solution for you! Here's a list of clever ways to help reinvigorate your career and find happiness in your job once again. You'll find plenty of tips to shake things up from our favorite experts, so come read along and get inspired!

Many people burn out on their jobs because they do the same thing day in and day out. It's important to rotate careers now and then and take on new jobs that will keep you energized and interested. Not only that, but it's important to get away from the same people all the time. It's easy for relationships to develop in the workplace, but they shouldn't be the center of your social life, so get out there and meet new people!

Whether you need a change of pace for your career or just some time off, it can be hard finding ways to make your job seem fresh and exciting. There is no such thing as "just one more day." If you've felt like you don't want to go to work tomorrow or that the last thing you want to do when you leave work today is going back the next day, it's time to stop struggling and start looking for a new line of work.

Job Burnout

When you burn out, it's easy to feel like that last job was the worst one you've ever had. The truth is that all of the jobs you've had have burned you out in a different way. It's important to understand how jobs burn us out to figure out how to avoid it ourselves.

The idea of burnout is becoming more and more pervasive in the workplace. It is said that every job will eventually lead to burnout if you have no change. In the past, people were more likely to get a new job as soon as they burned out on the old one. However, people are starting to realize that there are other alternatives if they don't want to continue their current job indefinitely.

When you're burned out at work, you aren't feeling fulfilled by your job. You may have a sense of dread when you think about going to work, or you may just feel emotionally exhausted without any understanding of why. If you find that you're always putting in your all at work — and yet it feels like your job never changes and never gets better — this can be a sign of burnout.

Most people get into this cycle because they think that if they put in more hours or try harder, their jobs will eventually become fulfilling in new and exciting ways. Unfortunately, this just isn't true at all. It's more likely that this is going to make burnout worse. Maybe it doesn't pay as well as you'd like, or corporate culture has become stagnant and boring. Whatever the case may be, there are ways to transform your career — even if your job is in the field of sales — so that you can feel happier and more fulfilled at work.

Possible causes of job burnout

There are some reasons why job burnout happens. The following are a few of them:

Lack of control

Things you don't have any control over are the ones that can make you feel tired and worn out. For example, maybe you work in a field where the company is constantly changing, and there aren't any benefits. You may not be able to do much about this, but you can at least try to have some sort of influence on your job. It's much better for your job satisfaction if you have control over things than if there's no control at all. Things you don't have any control over are the ones that can make you feel tired and worn out. You may not be allowed to set your hours, let alone what's required of you.

Unclear job expectations

Many jobs don't have clear job requirements. Instead, work is often filled with vague phrases like "make sure this happens" or "take this call." Your job will feel unclear until you start doing it. Many jobs don't have clear job requirements. Instead, work is often filled with vague phrases like "make sure this happens" or "take this call." Your job will feel unclear until you start doing it.

Lack of a path for success

Many people find that their jobs become sources of frustration because they can never figure out what success looks like.

Extremes of activity

Your job may have become so hectic that you're unable to find time to do the things you love. This can be a huge source of stress for people who love music, art, and literature.

Lack of social support

If you work in a competitive environment where the people you work with are constantly putting each other down, you're going to be feeling low and frustrated.

Work-life imbalance

This is one of the most common sources of job burnout. People find that they're spending all of their time at work and too much of their time away from work. This can make you feel like you have no social outlet when you get home from work.

Getting Past Burnout at Work

Some tips for getting past burnout at work:

<u>Change your job search tactics</u>: On paper, your job search should not look like burnout. You should be excited, energized, and ready to get the job done. There are, however, times when the simple things in life can take a back seat to work. If you've felt like you don't want to go to work tomorrow or that the last thing you want to do when you leave work today is going back the next day, it's time for a change.

<u>Get a job that requires your passion</u>: Maybe you've been searching for work that fits your passion. Maybe, you've been burned out on your current line of work because it only pays so much, or the culture has become stagnant. Whatever the case may be, there are many jobs out there that will satisfy your passion and give you a sense of purpose. Even if you aren't the most qualified candidate to get the job, look for something that will make up for any gaps in your resume and skillset.

<u>Schedule phone interviews and meetings</u>: Yes, you will have to do your research and look for the best position. And yes, this means that you might have to spend time doing something other than looking for work. But, if you've been feeling burned out at work, it's worth it. You can always schedule a few phone interviews or meeting through the course

of your job search — just stick to the scheduled appointments and don't cancel on anyone.

Seek out social roles: It's all too easy to become chained down by your job when you feel burnt out. When this happens, you can fall into unhealthy habits at work (like checking email or playing solitaire in meetings). Instead, seek out social roles in your job (like reading up on company events or joining a group for lunch) to keep things interesting and allow you to feel like you're engaged at work.

Ask people for advice about your job search: Asking the right people for advice about your job search will help to refuel your career and allow you to learn new things about the field and why it's important that you're happy at work.

Be flexible about your schedule: If you're feeling burnt out at work, it may look like there's no hope for your career. This is not the case. Being flexible and agile about your schedule will help you reinvent your role in your job search and let you remain open-minded regarding what's next for you professionally.

Take a sabbatical: Whether it's six months off or a year off, these "sabbaticals" will allow you to think about new opportunities while also providing relief from the stress of work. You can always come back from a sabbatical and get more traction on your career — or it doesn't have to be permanent!

Join a non-profit: Perhaps you've been thinking about ways to be more involved in the community. Maybe you want to support a cause or find a way to give back. To burn out less at work, it's helpful for you to consider volunteering at least part-time to gain experience and fluency in the field that interests you.

What's next: If you're feeling burnt out at work, it's time to look toward what's next. Maybe there's something you can do with your job to help make things better for yourself and everyone around you? Perhaps if there is something that isn't working for YOU, others need your help.

Take a break

When you're burnt out, you sometimes just need to take a break from your job. This is an opportunity for you to rest, reflect and use this time to decide if what you're doing at work is right for you or if it's time to start looking for something new.

The worst thing about burnout is not able to concentrate on the things that matter. When you get burned out, it means that you are overworked and could use some downtime. But on the contrary, there are some jobs where downtime can be devastating or dangerous — like those in medical professions or government jobs.

Change your job to escape burnout

Yes, changing your job will help you escape burnout. But you can do some things in your present job to avoid burnout. Some tips to avoid burnout while working

• Avoid focusing too much on work and instead, work smarter instead of harder.

• Try not to take your work home with you every day. It will allow you to stay focused and get more enjoyment out of the rest of your life.

• Find those small things in your job that you enjoy and do them often, even if it doesn't seem like it's part of the work that needs to be done.

• Avoid others' negative comments about your job. Criticism is a major stressor, so you will be able to relieve the stress in your job by avoiding it.

• Find time to rest; this will allow you to stay refreshed and focused on the tasks that need to be done.

• If you are about burnout, try to stay away from your work for a while or focus on something else such as hobbies, sports, and friends.

Many things can make it hard for people in their career at any age. So, what should you do if you're burnt-out or burnt-in? As with everything, the answer lies within yourself. Ask yourself these questions and decide on how to proceed in your own life:

· What am I feeling right now?

· How am I feeling?

· Why am I feeling that way?

These are the most important things to figure out when it comes to tackling the issue of burnout. You need to understand where you are mentally and emotionally before deciding on a course of action.

Method 22:
Get to the Root of the Problem

There are many reasons why people become emotionally and physically exhausted, but it is not always easy to identify the root cause. If you've ever been burnt out, you know how devastating it can be. You have trouble focusing on simple tasks, and the only thing that seems to give you any relief is sleep. But the damage doesn't stop there — burnout can eventually lead to total breakdown.

Burnout happens when we do too much with too little time and encouragement. It's usually caused by stress, fatigue, or a lack of control over how we work or live our lives. Fortunately, burnout is completely avoidable if you take some time to prioritize what is important in your life.

Identifying the root cause of the problem

– Do you ever feel like you're driving in circles? Your feelings of self-sabotage and impatience, overwhelming work demands, concern for the well-being of others, and your desire to succeed at all costs might not cause so much as symptoms. This chapter will explore what's going on when we experience burnout.

– It isn't always easy to identify our root problems — whether it be a lack of sleep, a sore body trying to tell us we've been sitting too long, or a deep-seated sense that something isn't right. Even seemingly insignificant triggers may land us right into the belly of the burnout beast. It's not always easy to know where we're going wrong, but this is undoubted because of how complex our brains are.

– To begin to unravel the complexities of burnout from a psychological perspective, it is necessary first to understand what burnout looks like on an emotional level. First off, different types of burnout affect us in different ways. For example, physical exhaustion and emotional exhaustion (perhaps more commonly known as "burned out", "exhausted", or "worn out") both feel similar but differ in how they manifest themselves in our bodies and emotions. Stress.

If you work at a stressful job or are experiencing other environmental stressors such as working long hours or living in cramped quarters, bringing them under control will help prevent burnout. Alternatively, if it's a matter of feeling overwhelmed by all the demands on you, take some time for yourself to relax and do something fun once in a while.

– Tiredness. When we're tired, our bodies and mind tend to make decisions that are not always in our best interests. If you feel increasingly exhausted or emotionally drained during the day, consider what is causing your fatigue.

– Lack of control over work conditions. We often take work conditions for granted and fail to see how they can be beneficial to us. Individuals who feel they've little control in their work environment are more vulnerable to burnout because these individuals don't make well-informed decisions in coping with the demands of their jobs. They usually take shortcuts and lack ongoing support, leading to emotional burnout.

– Overwork. If there's no time to rest or take care of oneself, it's very easy to get burned out. Try taking a vacation now and then and break away from the routine for a while. This will help you establish what matters in life, what is more, important than work, and how much you're willing to sacrifice on your job for other tasks.

– A lack of personal support. If you have no one at work or at home that you can turn to during difficult times, it's important to identify the root cause and seek outside support from someone who offers her time and support during bad times.

– Lack of regular feedback. Feedback is a powerful tool used by managers to measure the performance of their employees. Helping them identify strengths and weaknesses and provides employees with the necessary support. The feedback process is essential to help provide clarity and direction to individuals, thus increasing their motivation. If you're not receiving regular feedback from your boss, you may want to think about ways of getting that data or how you can get more support in the office.

There are ways to dealing with stress and fatigue:

– making physical changes such as eating well, taking exercise, or reducing alcohol intake.

– making emotional changes such as seeking social support from friends, family, or colleagues, attending therapy sessions, and maintaining a spiritual connection with life.

– making lifestyle changes such as putting self-care on the top of your list and removing yourself from toxic people or situations.

– adopting a more purposeful attitude towards work by trimming unnecessary tasks and reassessing priorities.

Eliminating the root cause

If you wish to eliminate burnout, it's important to identify the root cause first. Burnout is not a sign of defects or character flaws that you should be ashamed of but, rather, a sign of productive and healthy behavior. The key is to scrutinize your life and make adjustments before the problem turns into a disorder or causes you to sacrifice too much on your job.

– Give yourself time off. Even though many people believe they don't need it, taking care of yourself is vital. Take frequent breaks to do something you enjoy and recharge before starting the next part of your workday.

– Adjust your work and life schedule. If you have a lot of work, it's important to reduce your hours at work. If you are tired at night, take some time off or go to bed earlier before falling asleep. Sadly, many people continue working longer hours and even sacrifice their health and family life in the process. Don't let this happen to you!

– Identify what is important in your life, what matters more than money or career choices. You must realize that your health is more important than anything else in the world. Not everyone can afford to quit their jobs or stop working altogether to focus on their personal development because they have children or responsibilities to care for. Don't make the mistake of neglecting your health. Like any other relationship in life, nurturing your relationship with yourself means caring about what's good and bad for you and being honest about what you do and don't like.

– Identify the goals important to you. Visualizing progress towards your goals and forming a vision board containing pictures representing your aspirations helps keep you motivated when everything seems bleak. For example, if you want to move up the career ladder, speak with your boss about this goal and develop a plan to achieve it.

– Establish support systems such as attending therapy sessions, spiritual or religious gatherings. Gradually, you will start developing other relationships in your life and stop feeling so dependent on your job for self-worth.

– Don't neglect the emotional side of work. Make sure that you are heard by at least one manager or co-worker who will listen to your feedback and provide regular feedback of their own. Try to spend more time with people you enjoy being around, as this is the best way of eliminating stress and burnout.

By taking care of yourself and making these changes in your life, you can learn how to deal with the challenges thrown at you by life's circumstances.

Conclusion

It is difficult to combat burnout, but it's not impossible. The first step is to avoid it by recognizing its warning signs and taking action before things get too bad. Make time for yourself, take a break from work, and make some necessary changes. You're not alone in this – millions of people are feeling burnt out all around the world. And there is a way out!

It's not easy to stay motivated and productive when we're burnt out. It takes effort to get your head in the game and become a high-achiever again. But you can do it because you have lots of experience to draw on, and if you keep delaying or procrastinating on the things you need to do, then eventually, you'll end up getting them done.

You need that extra little bit of motivation. Where can you find it? Within yourself! Don't worry about other people; set aside time for yourself and do something enjoyable, which recharges your mental batteries and makes it easier for you to get back into the groove. You can also look for an outside source of motivation, such as a friend, a coach, or a mentor.

And don't forget to take time for yourself away from work. Not only do you soothe your soul by doing something relaxing, but it also gives you the chance to destress and clear your mind. There's nothing worse than spending hours at work and then having to get up early the next morning and do it all over again! You need to go easy on yourself as well. Don't expect to be super productive all the time: your mind needs time to recharge too.

Lightning Source UK Ltd.
Milton Keynes UK
UKHW020212080521
383350UK00003B/335